FAITH: ITS NATURE AND MEANING

Faith: its Nature and Meaning

Papers of the Maynooth Union Summer School 1970

EDITED BY
PAUL SURLIS

GILL AND MACMILLAN

First published in 1972

Gill and Macmillan Limited
2 Belvedere Place
Dublin 1
and in London through association with the
Macmillan
Group of Publishing Companies

Jacket/Cover designed by Graham Shepherd

7171 0587 3

Printing history: 10 9 8 7 6 5 4 3 2 1

Printed and bound in the Republic of Ireland by
Leinster Leader Ltd., Main Street, Naas, Co. Kildare

PAPERS OF THE
MAYNOOTH UNION SUMMER SCHOOLS

Mother of the Redeemer, edited by Kevin McNamara, Gill & Son: Dublin 1959; Sheed & Ward: New York 1960. Papers of the 1958 session.

Preaching, edited by Ronan Drury, Gill & Son: Dublin 1962; Sheed & Ward: New York 1963. Papers of the 1960 session.

Christian Unity, edited by Kevin McNamara, The Furrow Trust, Gill & Son: Dublin 1962. Papers of the 1961 session.

The Meaning of Christian Marriage, edited by Enda McDonagh, The Furrow Trust, Gill & Son: Dublin 1963; Alba House: New York 1964. Papers of the 1962 session.

Sacraments, edited by Denis O'Callaghan, The Furrow Trust, Gill & Son: Dublin 1964; Sheed & Ward: New York 1965. Papers of the 1963 session.

Moral Theology Renewed, edited by Enda McDonagh, The Furrow Trust, Gill & Son: Dublin 1965. Papers of the 1964 session.

The Meaning of the Church, edited by Donal Flanagan, Gill & Son: Dublin and Sydney 1966; *The Evolving Church*, Alba House: New York 1966. Papers of the 1965 session.

Sin and Repentance, edited by Denis O'Callaghan, Gill & Son: Dublin and Sydney 1967; Alba House: New York 1967. Papers of the 1966 session.

The Christian in his World, edited by Brendan Devlin, Gill & Son: Dublin and Sydney 1968. Papers of the 1967 session.

Understanding the Eucharist, edited by Patrick McGoldrick, Gill and Macmillan: Dublin and London 1969. Papers of the 1968 session.

Priest: Person and Ministry, edited by Gerard Meagher, Gill and Macmillan: Dublin and London 1970. Papers of the 1969 session.

CONTRIBUTORS

HENDRIKUS BERKHOF
  Professor of Systematic Theology, University of Leiden

DONAL J. DORR, M.A., D.D.
  Professor of Dogmatic Theology, St Patrick's College, Kiltegan

PIET FRANSEN, S.J.
  Professor of Dogmatic Theology, University of Louvain

FRANZ CARDINAL KOENIG, Archbishop of Vienna
  President of the Vatican Secretariat for Unbelievers

P. J. MCGRATH, M.A., PH.D.
  Professor of Metaphysics, St Patrick's College, Maynooth

JAMES P. MACKEY, D.D., PH.D.
  Lecturer in Theology, University of San Francisco

WILLIAM J. PHILBIN, D.D.
  Bishop of Down and Connor

PAUL SURLIS, D.D.
  Professor of Dogmatic Theology, St Patrick's College,
  Maynooth

Contents

Introduction

PAUL SURLIS

THE theology of faith has been somewhat neglected in the renewal and revitalization that have characterized other areas of theology in recent years. Apologetic and polemical concerns, on the one hand, and an impoverished view of revelation, on the other, had produced a theology of faith that was bloodless and abstract and frequently of little use, as it proved, in enabling people to accommodate themselves to sudden change, or to sustain the mood of radical questioning which is a feature of our time. But asking questions is a healthy exercise and asking the right questions is a necessary preliminary to advance in knowledge and understanding. What is more to be feared is an attitude of indifference, an agnostic stance that would shrug off religion with its debates and divisions as irrelevant, and would cease to ask questions because no worthwhile answers would be expected.

The best way to forestall such indifference is for theologians to face squarely the central issues involved in an adequate theology of faith and to propose answers to the questions so often repeated today: what is faith, is faith possible in a secularized world, how does faith relate to man's ordinary life and experience, and what does faith contribute to man's life? These and other questions occupied the Maynooth Summer School's thirteenth session in 1970 under the general heading 'Faith'. A complete theology of faith is not offered here, but what is offered goes to the heart of the matter.

Believers in God and in the Christian religion have always had to fight problems and overcome difficulties as Cardinal Koenig points out in 'Problems of Believing Today'. There have always been those who dismissed religion as illusion and others who were repelled from believing by the problem of evil. Problems of a qualitatively new sort are created for faith in a scientific and technological-oriented society in which man tends to see himself as sovereign of the world and shaper of its destiny. In the name of complete human autonomy belief in God is rejected. But Cardinal Koenig sees signs of hope: there is among scientists a new awareness of the non-objectifiable character of physical reality as witnessed by their discussion of scientific language in terms of image and symbol. Consequently there is a new sympathy for the images and symbols of religion which seek to express transcendent reality. And a new appreciation is being gained of religion itself as that alone which can undergird meaning and value in life as a whole. Cardinal Koenig, in fact, sees many of the problems facing believers today as really challenges which can eventually lead to a stronger and more purified faith.

Faith is a correlative of revelation and so the recent development and enrichment of the theology of revelation must be pressed into service in providing a more profound theology of faith. Revelation may be summarily described as the self-communication of God to the creature, but an expression like 'self-communication' can become a cliché unless something more precise is said about the form it takes and the human structures and realities through which it operates. Professor Fransen in 'Divine Revelation: Source of Man's Faith' tackles the relationship between grace, described in terms of divine indwelling of which man has a real if obscure experience, revelation and faith. He emphasizes the necessity of keeping man's social and language-using nature in mind when discussing grace and revelation since God in communicating himself to man respects man's nature and reaches his innermost depths through the two inter-related realities of language and community.

Faith is an act of the whole man and not simply intellectual assent to revealed propositions. What is the explanation, then, of the highly intellectualized accounts of faith given in texts emanating from Trent and Vatican I? James Mackey offers the necessary historical perspectives for evaluating the teaching on faith of the Councils referred to, in the introductory part of his paper, 'Christian Faith as Personal Response'. Despite the complex of attitudes and responses which is covered by the word 'faith' in the Bible, Mackey finds and illustrates an inherent logic and development in the broad range of meaning. He proceeds from biblical and traditional understandings of faith to elaborate a theology of faith as acknowledgement and trust, the response to an invitation which comes to every man from God in his concrete historical existence. Faith makes claims on the whole man, and what these claims are in the case of Christian faith is dealt with.

Despite the frequency with which the word 'experience' occurs in theological writing about God and faith today, experience—and particularly anything claiming the title 'religious experience'—was distrusted in Catholic theology until recent times. The expression was vaguely felt to be associated with capitulation before the arguments of Hume and Kant concerning the capacity of human reason in reaching natural knowledge of God. Appeal to religious experience was felt to be a dubious substitute for certain knowledge and ultimately a weak apologetic for religion. But the problems with which theology is wrestling today make it obvious that a study of the theologians of religious experience is indispensable even if their teaching on certain crucial matters must be rejected. Donal Dorr in 'Religious Experience and Christian Faith', isolates what is of permanent value in the writings of Otto, Schleiermacher and some Modernists, and he argues carefully to a solution that is philosophically and theologically more adequate than theirs to the problem of the objectification of religious experience.

Controversies regarding the nature of faith were one of the great divisive issues of the Reformation. Comparison of the theology of faith advanced by the Reformers with the prevailing theology against which they reacted, shows that their major concern was to personalize the understanding of faith, indeed of the whole of doctrine. In 'The Act of Faith in the Reformed Tradition', Professor H. Berkhof, well-known theologian and author, and a member of the Reformed Church, analyses the Reformers' teaching on faith and traces its subsequent development. On the basis of close analysis of present-day Catholic and Reformed teaching on faith he states that the two traditions have never been as close as they are at present, a conclusion of deep ecumenical significance, remaining disagreements referring to the context in which faith functions rather than to faith itself.

The insistence in contemporary theology and in some of the documents of the Second Vatican Council, that true faith in God is a possibility outside the Church raises several important questions: what is the origin and nature of this faith, does its being a possibility for all men render the Church unnecessary, and if not what is the role of the Church with reference to this faith? Addressing himself to the topic 'The Historical Church as Mediator of Faith' Mackey develops further the understanding of faith expressed in his first paper. He affirms the possibility of faith for all men, and shows how the commitment which it involves receives further and higher specification when faith (or basic faith) becomes Christian faith. Basic faith is intensely personal and dynamic and possesses its own in-built criteria which permit the assessment of certain Church procedures and structures which may, when outmoded, hinder rather than promote faith.

The relationship between faith and reason is important, as the history of theology shows. The Church rejects Fideism and Traditionalism as firmly as she rejects Rationalism. Esteem for revelation is never allowed to lead to disparagement of reason. Theological and anthropological issues of deep significance are at stake in discussions concerning faith and reason, consequently assumptions and presuppositions must be carefully examined so that false claims may be avoided and impossible demands are not made as they have been, for example, in the realm of certainty and proof. In this whole discussion, as Patrick J. McGrath shows in his paper 'Faith and Reason', it is necessary to have an adequate theology of revelation, and a correct understanding of where the rationality and certainty of faith are to be located so that the problem of the relationship between faith and reason may be correctly stated. It is only then that a solution may be offered which does justice on the one hand to faith, understood as response to divine revelation in its present actuality and on the other hand, to human reason accepted as it normally exists and operates.

During a period of transition and change, such as the present, it is imperative for Christians to know what is distinctive about their religion, so that in any process of re-interpretation which may be found necessary, nothing of value will be jettisoned. Christianity is a divinely revealed religion, and it makes demands in the intellectual and moral spheres to which man's response must be characterized especially by faith and obedience. In the concluding paper, 'The Way of Faith', Bishop William J. Philbin deals with these and other themes as he delineates the essential features of the Christian religion. 'The conveying of knowledge and of power directly from God is what constitutes Christianity'. He warns that any form of reductionism or misrepresentation in any of the key-areas of Christianity would do inestimable damage to the faith itself and to the life it is meant to inspire.

The main lines along which the theology of faith is being renewed and developed are already clear, as the papers in this collection endeavour to show. It is clear too that the problems still awaiting solution are becoming more clearly defined. Among them are the production of new forms of credal statement in which the essence of the traditional faith will be expressed in terms intelligible to modern man, and the provision of a theology in which both personal commitment and devotion and the social role and implications of the faith will be underpinned. Despite the impressive work which has been done it is clear that we still await a theology of revelation in which due attention is given also to the literary genres other than historical writing in the Bible. In the matter of the relationship between faith and the Church the continuing necessity of the Church and missionary endeavour must be clearly maintained, while the possibility of true faith existing outside the Church is investigated. And there is the problem of atheism and disbelief. Atheism is sometimes a response evoked by distorted belief which hides rather than reveals the true face of God. The response to atheism is the example of faith intensely lived. The first step towards the life of faith which makes 'God the Father and his Incarnate Son present and in a sense visible'[1] is correct understanding, but understanding is only the first step and it is finally in the integral life of faith that its nature and meaning begin to be adequately grasped.

Problems of Believing Today

FRANZ KOENIG

MY topic concerns the contemporary problems encountered by people who believe in and profess the Christian faith. This theme refers, at least indirectly, to the field of studies and activities of the Secretariate for Unbelievers with which I am associated. Now, I do not intend to describe the work of that Secretariate here, but I should like to observe that although my involvement in it takes me all round the world and brings me into contact with many 'unbelievers' I could recite many instances, known to me personally, of individuals who may be classed as 'unbelievers' but are in fact dissatisfied with unbelief. In my visits behind the Iron Curtain, to take but one example, I have met people who, despite being official members of the Marxist party, were deeply dissatisfied with its inability to answer for them the questions which deal with the ultimate problems of life, its meaning and purpose. Scepticism exists with regard to the validity of the unbeliever's position and I have heard envy expressed for the peace of mind and contentment of those who believe.

My present task is not to discuss the problem of unbelief in itself but to present the problems which confront the believer today. In what follows I shall try to show that there are certain difficulties for the Christian which originate in the essence of faith itself and which have always been the subject of apologetic or dogmatic discussion in one form or another. Secondly, I shall discuss in greater detail the essential problems sharply posed for the believer by our contemporary situation. Thirdly, I shall draw attention to positive factors which today are capable of eliminating obstacles to belief and so help to confirm the believer in his positive decision and attitude.

Problems intrinsic to belief

Ignorance of the faith or imperfect understanding of its meaning and implications have always posed problems with which catechetical instruction and pastoral care have endeavoured to cope. It has always been understood that personal behaviour and moral attitudes may foster the inner disposition for faith, or, when they are evil, they may militate against and destroy this disposition. One aspect of faith—that it is an act of obedience—is stressed in Romans (1:5), and Vatican I, has taught that this obedience means total submission to the authority of the revelation of God. Voluntary submission of this nature is obviously greatly influenced by the total way of life of the individual.

Another difficulty has always resulted from the fact that man's deepest striving is for insight, understanding and comprehension. But in faith man is confronted with God as a mystery the comprehension of which exceeds man's powers of understanding. Lord Russell in his day emphasized the fact that man strives for clarity and rejects mysteries whether metaphysical or theological. Moreover, man is free and the act of faith must also be freely made. God does not compel the assent of faith (which when it is given, he enables without destroying its freedom), and so man may refuse to believe.

Then there are the objections urged against any faith or religion making claims to be directed to an absolute and transcendent personal being on whom the world is said to depend. Democritus is the forerunner of those who regard religion as the product of human fear and insecurity, and who see in the promises of religion merely projections of the human mind in the face of an almost insufferable existence. We are familiar with the use Marx made of this theme and with his attacks on religion which, he argued, was used by the ruling classes to keep their subjects passive and submissive. Science and reason, it was confidently expected, would satisfactorily answer the 'ultimate' questions for which God as a hypothesis was unnecessary.

Problems of evil

The problem of the existence of evil and suffering has always posed one of the greatest difficulties to religious belief, and specifically to the Christian religion which claims that God is all-powerful, wise and loving. Either God can solve the problem of evil and remove suffering and he will not (in which case he is not a God of love), or he is incapable of solving the problem of evil (in which case he is not all-powerful, no longer God). This dilemma is no academic matter, as personal suffering and widely publicized atrocities and disasters almost daily testify. The doctrine of the Fatherhood of God is put severely to the test for many, especially for those who, to begin with, are weak in faith and do not realize the incomprehensible greatness of the Creator and the absence of the creature's right to question God and demand an account from him (something which Job learned after wrestling with the problem of evil).

Desire for freedom

There is no doubting the fact that a fundamental difficulty against faith arises from the human desire for total independence and for absolute autonomy, both of which seem incompatible with recognizing God and his claims on man's life. Rebellion against the divine will and its commands is a theme already emphasized in the Genesis account of the Fall as is the related theme of the creature's turning from God and towards the world. What we may at least call a sense of the existence of God has been possessed by man since the beginning but present also has been the refusal to *acknowledge* God explicitly. And thus man falls back on himself, on his own world which, while it may also threaten, fascinates and allures him, and offers itself as his salvation.

Contemporary problems

The problems of believing peculiar to our age create, even within the Catholic Church, a climate inimical to faith and difficulties of a qualitatively new sort. We may begin with the progress of science and technology and a new sense of the world and its culture from which our typically modern problems arise.

Technological and scientific progress seem to offer previously unimagined opportunities for changing and planning the world, and this includes the biological sphere. More and more man

appears to be achieving the capacity to create his own future and
take his destiny into his own hands. As man's power thus
increases God recedes to an ever-increasing degree. The need for
God is no longer clear: science and progress can advance without
him, the 'God of the gaps' is no longer needed. And so modern
man finds himself with many varieties of secular humanism. Marx
stated its programme when he said that while in former days
philosophers contemplated the world, the task now was to change
the world. The Marxist believes that he can change the world by
his action, so that ultimately all men will live happily in a har-
monious world. A consequence of this is that abstract truths no
longer claim man's interest and the emphasis is put on facts that
can be verified experimentally. Former methods of knowledge
are discredited and experience alone is thought to provide
certainty, and give knowledge a secure basis.

With technological thinking and planning looking to the future,
as they do, the past becomes devoid of interest. Aversion from
the past is typical of our time and cannot be without influence
on the truth of Christianity which has historic foundations. There
is a genuine theological difficulty here which we do not wish to
overlook: theological doctrine has been formulated for the most
part in the so-called pre-scientific epoch, and this can contribute
towards making the language of the theologian unintelligible to
the scientist. There is the further fact that Scholasticism expounded the contents of the faith with reference to a particular
cosmic system and world-view. And while this was to some extent
also true of Protestantism, the biblical message of faith was less
clearly connected with a particular cosmic system in Protestantism
than was the case in Catholic theology.

Freedom and authority

Much of the dialogue between Christianity and the modern
world concentrates on the problems of freedom. The striving for
ever greater freedom is one of the main characteristics of our
time which regards freedom as among the highest secular values.
Out of the striving for freedom, conflicts of many different sorts
arise: the different kinds of contemporary atheism are the consequences of a thorough-going affirmation of freedom. From

Nietzsche to Sartre the negation of God seems to result from the conviction that if God's existence is affirmed and acknowledged then man loses his freedom and independence. In order to achieve the liberation of man, the right to force and revolution is frequently asserted today. Difficult moral decisions have to be made concerning the legitimacy of the use of force, and conflict with the Church sometimes occurs.

Freedom from authority is often demanded and to such an extent that one may speak of a world-wide crisis of authority as being characteristic of the age in which we live. The authority of the Church is challenged in the name of freedom as are her teaching mission and her personal role. Charism and freedom are emphasized at the expense, often, of the institution, and the self-sufficiency of the local community is asserted against the claims of higher authority. Demands are made for pluralism of theology and of morals. It is argued that 'the anonymous Christian' can find a place in the Church. At times one cannot fail to see a reduction of Christianity to humanism and an ignoring of the specific meaning of what it is to be Christian.

It must be stated that freedom as a value is ambivalent: freedom is one of man's noblest qualities but the temptation to abuse freedom is as great as the desire for freedom. It is the mission of the Catholic Church today—to put the matter positively—to make modern man aware that freedom leads to positive development only where there is also inner commitment to values, to truth, and, above all, commitment to man in love. Otherwise, freedom may only unleash blind, destructive forces.

A related problem arises from the discovery of the relative autonomy of the world and a deeper appreciation of its values which are: freedom, community, peace and solidarity. They appear to be attainable by human means and not to require religious foundations. Doctrine and belief seem to be irrelevant. And while modern, secular man may retain a desire to believe he presupposes that all the values of the world retain their phenomenal meaning. The world is meant to become, as it were, the appearance of God. This way lie pantheism and forms of Gnosticism which stand in marked contrast to the Christian doctrine of creation with its clear distinction between Creator and creature and its nuanced teaching on the transcendence and immanence of God.

If the world and the profane are regarded as absolutely autonomous, the world becomes an idol, total submission to which leads to disappointment, desolation and finally, a complete void. By its dark elements and its obscurities the world shows that it is not ultimate and that it cannot provide man's ultimate and absolute happiness.

Science and religion

The conflict between science and religion is no longer as sharp as formerly. Here, I refer to the human rather than to the natural sciences and to the conflict which may arise between religion and, for example, psychology, psychoanalysis, sociology and anthropology. The nub of the problem is that what is put forward by believers as religious aspiration and experience is sometimes interpreted by practitioners of the above-mentioned disciplines as human projection or simply as a product of human desire for comfort, security, affection, power, vengeance and so on. Therefore the question arises today: if you eliminate all these elements what will remain of religious faith? Psychology and sociology are beginning to claim a loud voice in the field of religion, and positive achievements will, doubtless, be of great benefit. But a religion which is interpreted solely on the basis of psychological, psychoanalytical or sociological analysis will have its true nature destroyed if the limited competence of these sciences is not kept in mind and if the unique nature of religion is ignored.

Spirit of criticism and doubt

We come now to discuss the spirit of criticism and doubt which pervades religion and faith: scepticism towards many positions and values of the past is expressed. Problems are emphasized but no solutions are offered. And, by virtue of this spirit of doubt and criticism, faith is brought into a situation of conflict. For faith is the strong conviction of things that cannot be seen. If everything is doubted how can faith survive? A radically sceptical attitude—even, it seems, on the part of some theologians—is manifested towards all the mysteries of the faith. The doctrines in question concern the personal nature of God, revelation,

Scripture as the inspired word of God, the teaching authority of the Church and dogmatic and moral principles.

It should be observed, however, that the spirit of criticism and scepticism also extends to the new authority of science and to an uncritical confidence in progress. For in this field, too, one cannot verify everything and one is compelled to trust without seeing. And yet this is no advantage for the faith; rather, it leads to an intensification of general scepticism. Formerly, somewhat worried or arrogantly, one doubted single dogmas; today scepticism is applied to faith and to everything that must be acknowledged by virtue of authority. A positive aspect can, perhaps, be found in this universal scepticism. Scientific findings in detail hardly entail any danger for faith today. Also the problems of evil and suffering tend to diminish in importance as an argument against faith in God. The opinion is found in our day that it might be possible to eliminate evil and suffering from the world by the expenditure of more energy and money. Such is the technical mentality of man today.

Exegetical problems

Catholic exegesis in recent years has become a source of new problems for believers, perhaps especially since the conclusion of Vatican II, which, within certain justifiable limits, has approved the new exegetical methods of modern biblical scholarship. Catholic exegetes have relatively recently begun to deal with problems which have exercised Protestant exegetes for a much longer period of time. Modern interpretation of the Scriptures is having its repercussions within the theological and ecclesiastical fields and, some would add, is causing confusion.

The fact that we are better informed nowadays about the development of the books of the Bible, about the time of their origin, and about their position within their cultural environment—'form criticism'—does not necessarily call in question the Bible as message of God, as it is handed on to us by the tradition of the Church. Hand in hand with this historical criticism goes the material criticism, which is called demythologizing and which tries to do a service for modern man, who cannot believe any more in the spirits or the world of miracles of the New Testament.

It seeks to help him by detecting the hidden elements of truth and the proper meaning in all the mythical formulations. In its extreme form this leads to the belief that all statements of the Bible are nothing more than symbols and images in which man attempts to express the experiences of his life. In this case nothing is left of the decisive historical facts of the work of Redemption.

However, the latest findings of Bible scholars often differ very widely: 'The results of the analysis of form criticism vary according to the different scholars.' And the reason for this lies in subconscious attitudes and presumptions. It is based upon the various extra-exegetical systems of ideas of the different exegetes or on the philosophic presuppositions, sometimes active at the subconscious level, which may influence the exegete in his work. Such contradictory results of exegesis enable us to understand why the 'authentic interpretation of the Holy Scriptures' has been entrusted to the Church as a kind of essential service. Therefore everyone who does not trust in the teaching authority of the Church goes astray even when, indeed precisely when, he is a theologian.

Linguistic problems

Linguistic philosophy has revealed to us the community aspect of the understanding of truth. But language as mediation of faith raises new problems: how far can revealed truth be rendered and formulated with linguistic accuracy? The listening of man and the understanding of the listener present yet other problems. It is here that one may find the roots of many questions of exegesis today. Added to all this is the fact that the teaching authority exists as intermediary between the Scriptures and the faithful. Here the question arises of how far the teaching authority formulates doctrine with accuracy in order to be heard and understood correctly in the changing course of time.

Witness to the faith

A further uncertainty seizes the faithful today when they realize that many non-believers—be they materialists, agnostics or convinced atheists—are trying to lead morally irreproachable lives and are striving for high ethical standards. Moreover, it is observed that they frequently expend all their energies on behalf of others who are in distress or who need help. The efforts of such people for a more just and humane social order are very often admirable. Perplexity in face of such observations is still greater if one encounters believers who are egotistic or lead otherwise questionable lives. Furthermore, the question is raised whether religion in general and Christianity in particular might not be only the tradition of a particular epoch of culture, only a form of social order or an impulse from the subconscious.

Facts such as these together with the linguistic difficulties lead to the problem of witness to faith. Beginning with the New Testament, faith is necessarily dependent on witness and testimony. Whoever bears witness to his faith must also speak the language of his listeners. Therefore faith as a dialogue is subject to the changes of time and culture. And here the question arises: what is subject to change in the Christian message and what is unchangeable? This is the problem of the identity of faith, an identity maintained through ever-changing times.

Intensification and dissemination of problems

We conclude our short sketch of the problems and difficulties of believing today with a brief reference to the intensification and wider dissemination of these problems by the mass-media, by the coexistence of faith and unbelief, and of faithful and heretics within the Church.

The mass-media have produced the well-informed society of today. This informed society reacts more sharply to conflicts and thus renders them more acute. Public opinion exerts a strong pressure on the preacher and on the contents of what is preached.

The informed believers of today rightly express a desire to participate in the development of teaching in the Church and to have a say in the making of decisions by the ecclesiastical authority. As soon as a democratization of the Church—within given limits—came under discussion, the hitherto silent *unbelievers*, or those who were uncertain of their faith, began to join in the discussions within the Church and to present their doubts. Thus the uncertain and doubting members of the faithful—even the non-believers—are now sharing in the forming of public opinion and claim the right to have a voice in whatever discussions may be going on. The total number of uncertain people and of unbelievers now acts as a constant pressure in areas of faith and morals. The *sensus fidelium* and the *sensus infidelium* are now forming the public opinion within the Church and so the resonance of problems and difficulties in believing is intensified.

The frequent appearance of people who appear to profess heretical beliefs within the Church is a further aggravating factor especially since such people choose today to remain in the Church rather than leave it, as they should do, when and if they profess heretical doctrine. But they do not leave because they believe that they are anticipating the course which will be taken by the true doctrine of the Church of the future. They argue that the Church belongs to them and that their opponents are reactionaries and antiquated in their thinking. This remaining within the Church, as I have described it, intensifies the crisis of believing and gives greater resonance to its effects. Space does not permit me to develop at this point the theology of the guiding mission of the Church which in these circumstances assumes greater importance than ever.

Positive aspects of the present situation

I should now like to indicate some of the more important *positive* aspects of the present situation and to review their implications and the possibilities which they offer for Christian faith and religious life in our time. I am fully convinced that, despite the many difficulties and problems which I have enumerated, there is not less faith in existence today than in former periods of the history of mankind. Only the context within which faith is exercised, but not the faith itself, has changed. The questions today are: who is the true believer? what, and under what circumstances, does he believe? what consequences does he draw from his faith and how does he draw them?

Tradition and change

Balancing the many calls for revolution and a certain tendency to absolutize progress we find today a new appreciation of the meaning, necessity and importance of tradition. In a recent book

J. Pieper has shown convincingly that tradition is not a relic of the past but rather the fertile ground essential to the production of a humane existence.[1] Just as the individual, if he is not mentally disturbed, lives in the continuity of his existence, so also do peoples, states and institutions. In the dialectic of tradition and revolution lies a secret law of life of the world of western culture. Absolutism of progress and of revolution, and the holding all tradition in contempt, are forms of infidelity towards oneself and towards one's community and institutions.

From quite another point of view comes the warning of the biologist and behaviourist K. Lorenz against futile attempts to ignore or destroy all tradition. Generalizing from his insights into animal life and speaking about modern human problems he states: '. . . great ethical and moral confusion [can be caused when] the extremists of the younger generation think they should throw overbroad absolutely everything that has been handed on to them by their parental tradition, and [when] they indulge in the proud but false idea that they are able to build up a totally new culture on their own resources. At the same time they do not realize that they are doing their best, speaking in terms of cultural history, to fall back to the level of a hypothetical pre-palaeological period.' And he goes on to describe the reaction of stubborn adherence to tradition (even out-moded ones) which this extreme attitude on the part of the young can cause in members of the older generation.[2]

An acute assessment of the problem of tradition and change as it affects the Church has been provided by Fr. Bernard Lonergan who diagnoses the present crisis in the Church as being a crisis not of *faith* but of *culture*. Lonergan speaks of the breakdown of classical culture which, he says, 'cannot be jettisoned without being replaced; and what replaces it, cannot but run counter to classical expectations'. He then warns against hardening of attitudes and gives in a nutshell a programme for effecting the necessary transition from classical to modern culture: 'There is bound to be formed a solid right that is determined to live in a world that no longer exists. There is bound to be formed a scattered left, captivated by now this, now that new development, exploring now this and now that new possibility.

But what will count is a perhaps not numerous centre, big enough to be at home in both the old and the new, painstaking enough to work out, one by one, the transitions to be made, strong enough to refuse half-measures and insist on complete solutions even though it has to wait.'[3]

The bewildering speed of modern developments, however, raises the question: how much time is, from the human point of view, left for our renewal? Some (enemies of the Church and of Christianity) regard the conflicts within the Church as the beginning of its dissolution. The German atheist Gerhard Szcesny thinks the time has come to destroy the privileges which Christian Churches still enjoy in Germany. Indeed he maintains (somewhat self-contradictorily in view of his above-mentioned aim) that there is no longer any identifiable antagonist for the critic who wishes to address himself to Christianity.

Testimonies to belief in God

While it may be true that still further positions are destined to break down—positions which we today regard as indispensable —I remain convinced that present developments give plenty of grounds for hope and confidence. There is first of all the fact that in this period of an 'eclipse of God' (Buber) testimonies have appeared which, against all the 'God-is-dead sentiment', bear witness to encounters with God and to conversions which cannot in any way be reduced to purely human phenomena. That such events have aroused considerable and fairly widespread interest is also significant. I am thinking specifically here of André Frossard who was an atheist and a socialist and the story of whose conversion has now been translated into all the European languages and even reached the best-seller lists.[4] Another such book is that written by the actor Roger Boutefeu, also a former atheist. After what may be described as an 'inner encounter with Christ' the author spent eleven years as a shepherd leading a life of contemplation and prayer, and then decided to enter the Catholic Church.[5] Books such as these encourage the faithful and strengthen their religious convictions. Moreover, testimonies which are so obviously sincere cannot be ignored by unbelievers.

Belief in progress?

It is increasingly more obvious that *doubt about*, rather than *belief in*, progress better defines modern man's attitude to technical and scientific progress, the ambiguity of which is now clearly perceived. Man today sees himself confronted inescapably with the negative, noxious and potentially world-destroying effects of developments for which he himself is responsible. We all live under the threat of atomic war and awareness of this fact is always somewhere in the background of our thinking.

There is also the consideration that social and racial conflicts flare up with a new and unimagined bitterness. One part of mankind is endangered by hunger, another is threatened by pollution of the environment, everywhere there are calls of alarm. What is pressingly needed is a new ethic which will be aimed at the prevention of over-population and which will be designed to educate people in the exercise of control in consumption.

In an age when a multiplicity of factors operates to exclude religious experience and a sense of the transcendent, one must also refer to the strong inclination among modern youth towards prayer and meditation. Indeed, it is deplorable that there are so few teachers competent to introduce them in an adequate manner to the Christian tradition of mental prayer and its rich heritage of mystical theology. The 'flight into intoxication', evident among drug takers and social drop-outs, is for many a flight from the feeling of absurdity. The Viennese psychiatrist Frankl (founder of a new school of psychotherapy), emphasizes constantly that man today is 'existentially frustrated' because his purpose in life, his 'desire for meaning' is not fulfilled. This attitude of frustration with life is spreading more and more (even, as we have seen at the outset, behind the Iron Curtain), and Frankl traces its cause to man's loss of a sense of tradition that would give him orientation and provide his life with meaning.

Frankl sees a possible remedy for man's situation in an education of conscience towards responsibility, which will enable man to meet the challenges that confront him.[6] It is obvious that the posing of the question of the meaning and purpose of life can be the prelude to serious consideration of the claims of religion and the value systems and moral codes associated with it.

In the Marxist sphere the insight is dawning that the anthropology of Marxism has important shortcomings. The question is raised whether Marxist teaching can simply pass over 'those private questions of guilt, suffering, death and meaning, those ultimate questions which Christianity has been concerned with for over two thousand years'. Solutions, other than the Marxist one, to the nature and meaning of life are being discussed and consideration of Christian teaching concerning the 'mystery' of man is not excluded. The German Marxist and social philosopher Horkheimer has recently broken a lance for theology with his discussion of transcendence and cautious identification of the absolute with 'the Other'. He has argued that everything connected with morals leads to theology and not to secular considerations in the final analysis. Horkheimer has painted a gloomy picture of the totally manipulated society which the future may bring: a world without free will, a world without love—in a word, a boring world. He argues that should theology be abolished, then at the same time *meaning* will disappear from the world, and activity without purpose will prevail. But even if Horkheimer regards sombre developments (which we have only sketched here) as inevitable, he also considers it possible to salvage something of the traditional values based on religion by pointing to the *negative* nature of the change which excludes or dismisses them.[7]

Modern scientists and religious claims

Much that is promising has emerged recently in the field of science and especially in the realm of modern physics. The atomic physicist and Nobel prizewinner, Werner Heisenberg, in a book published recently, describes conversations held with colleagues concerning the relation between science and religion.[8] He states that the discovery of the theory of relativity and of the quantum theory have forced the exact sciences to give up the ideal of an objective world that follows the laws of causality within space and time. It was precisely the narrowness of this ideal which created conflict and scepticism regarding the spiritual element in religion. In modern scientific theory, Heisenberg continues, every physical fact comprises objective and subjective features. Modern physicists have also realized that in the description of the phenomena of quantum mechanics they can only speak in images and symbols, which do not correspond to reality but only approximate to it. Thus a new sympathy is born for the images and symbols of religion which offer the only possibility of expressing realities beyond the power of speech. Heisenberg argues that the narrow vision of positivism must be relegated to the past, and the exact sciences, while yielding none of their rigour in method or clarity of expression, must not dismiss as unreal the dimensions of reality which lie outside their fields of study. Heisenberg writes that if one raises elementary moral questions 'one always finds again the Christian standards of values' even where it is no longer easy or possible to understand the images and symbols of that religion.

Moral and spiritual values are as real as the forces and fields of energy with which science deals and life from which these values are ignored or in which they are suppressed can yield things 'worse than concentration camps and the atom bomb'. However, Heisenberg does not wish to dwell on the 'dark side of our world' but he does call for an appreciation on the part of science of the values and standards by which life as a whole must be directed.

Such, in broad outlines, are the positive aspects of the contemporary situation, aspects which indicate openness to reception of the Church's message and her gift of faith—faith comprising hope and charity too—which is the Church's only gift to the world, for which she is responsible before God.

The attitude of faith

Joseph Ratzinger has said that Christian belief 'means opting for the view that what cannot be seen is more real than what can be seen. It is an avowal of the primacy of the invisible as truly real, which bears us up and hence enables us to face the visible in a calm and relaxed way—knowing that we are responsible before the invisible as the true ground of all things.'[9] This attitude is an affront to the 'attitude which the present world situation seems to force us to adopt. In the face of positivism and phenomenalism it invites us to confine ourselves to the "visible" and the "apparent" in the widest sense of the terms; to extend the basic attitude to which natural science is indebted for its successes to the totality of our relationship with reality'.[10]

There are still problems, of course, in presenting the traditional faith in language intelligible today. There are attempts, and the Dutch Catechism is one example, which represent progress even if they are not satisfactory in every respect. But if we are genuinely open to the problems of the world, to the needs and doubts of modern man, then with the assistance of prayer and meditation on the word of God, and with help from the theologians, we shall be led forward by the Holy Spirit to the new expression of the faith which is required today. Nor must we forget that the message of faith must be verified by the life of the Church and of its individual members. Convincing testimony is given only by brotherhood and true community living which, however, are destined to fail unless they are rooted in the brotherhood of Christ and live by his power. Testimony is also given by liturgy that is living, meaningful and reverent before the mysteries which it celebrates. It is precisely in a pluralistic and secular society that the need is greater for places, ceremonial and ritual which foster man's sense of the transcendent and create an awareness of the nearness and relevance of the City of God in the cities of man.

We have outlined some of the problems which face believers today. It is well for people to be aware of the extent and precise nature of the conflicts and crises which exist. The distinction, for example, between a crisis of *faith* and a crisis of *culture* can be of enormous benefit to the faithful in understanding many of the changes which are taking place today and in locating the area where these changes are occurring. We have also considered other dimensions of the whole question of contemporary faith and its difficulties, and in all this we have tried to take account, too, of the positive hopeful factors in the overall situation.

Some people react to the modern crisis with fear and foreboding. But fear is not a good adviser. It is far better to realize that enormous challenges awaken new and frequently heroic powers of response; God's grace still abounds and for this let us be thankful. May our era not resemble the period after the

French Revolution when, in response to attack and the prospect of dissolution, new orders arose and men of powerful spirit and deep faith appeared in the Church? Without in any way yielding to false optimism we may be confident because there are many good things to be seen emerging today. There is a profound desire for justice, sincerity and truth. There is genuine growth in true freedom; it is good to see that many servile attitudes have been laid aside. There is growth in personal, genuine faith which is more than the product of custom and environment. There is an awakening of true commitment in the Church, and in the Churches, and there is the most encouraging sign of the denominations coming closer together.

The problems of believing today are, then, a challenge which if met with confidence will produce a Christian faith that will be deeper, more genuine and more compelling.

Divine Revelation: Source of Man's Faith

PIET FRANSEN

It is a well-known fact that in every religious tradition the adherents in one way or another believe that the Godhead has manifested his will or his wisdom to men or to a community, very often through the mediation of a religious founder or prophets. But Judaism, Islam and Christianity are forms of religion in which the acceptance of the free initiative of God in addressing himself to men, constitutes one of the fundamental characteristics of their faith. These religions stand or fall on the truth of a divine revelation.

The inborn and almost constitutional weaknesses and dangers of Christianity confirm this very basic truth. Christians, like Jews and Moslems for that matter, are more open than the adherents of other known forms of religion to either legalism or funda-mentalism. Both trends show indeed a very dangerous corruption of the true religious attitude itself. Nevertheless they seem quite common, eventually in a more or less latent way. Actually both are depraved forms of the belief that God has in fact revealed his decrees or his purpose or mind to the religious community, the Church. The corruption evidently does not lie in the accept-ance itself of this manifestation of God, but in the distortion of this faith. Legalism and formalism misuse a simplified and man-made version of the divine word to establish their own inner security, one of the deepest cravings of men, even against the 'insecurity' of the living God. They short-circuit, as it were, the tension between the radical absoluteness of God himself and the many man-made expressions of it in law and doctrine.

Is revelation possible?

Nowadays, under the influence of the biblical, the liturgical and the ecumenical movements, we have become even more familiar and almost careless with such ways of speaking, as 'we are listening to the word of God', 'we witness to his word', 'we stand by God's word', and many others. But very few, it appears to me, even among theologians and biblical scholars, seem to bother about explaining the meaning of this kind of language. Though this language has become rather fashionable, indeed, it is by no means self-explanatory. We use it too easily as a convenient cliché.

To make us aware of the problem, it suffices to quote a few statements from the New Testament itself. St John writes in his Prologue quite definitely: 'No one has ever seen God; it is the only Son, who is nearest to the Father's heart, who has made him known' (*John* 1:18). St Paul says of Christ: 'He is the image of the unseen God' (*Col.* 1:15). And in the first epistle to Timothy we read: 'The King of kings and the Lord of lords, who alone is immortal, whose home is in inaccessible light, whom no man has seen and no man is able to see' (1 *Tim.* 6:15-16).

These three statements all stress the radical need of the coming and the mediation of Christ among us so that we might come to know God as such, for God is unapproachable by man. Under the influence of Greek culture, which saw all kinds of knowledge in terms of vision and light, not excluding, however, the genuine Hebrew tradition which believed that no man could see God's face without dying (*Exod.* 33:20), the writers of the New Testament try to express the mystery of God's transcendence through the symbols of light and vision. But we could, as easily, say with the same radicality: no man has ever heard God's voice, for he speaks an inaudible language!

This conviction of God's invisibility and inaudibility, that is of his escaping the assimilating power of our mind, is still quite common to the tradition, theological and spiritual, of the Eastern Churches. One might even say that no serious theologian in our Western Church ever lost this deep awareness of God's depth and height. Especially, I would say, in our modern technical age we should remain conscious of this. Knowledge entails for our contemporaries the ability to manipulate and to master the objects we know. We should realize that that kind of knowledge of God is radically impossible to attain. The God whom we would know in that way would be inevitably a man-made idol. To dream that we might be able to manipulate God, as we unconsciously do in a magical attitude and in the more subtle way of ritualism and legalism, means that we are implicitly introducing God within the ambit of the earthly powers we hope to conquer. This was only done in some forms of decadent theology, as e.g. the more rationalistic scholastic theology of the nineteenth century, which lost the true sense of God's majesty in its self-confident and naïve conceptual speculation.

My intention in this paper is to try to show *how* God reveals himself to us. And when I saw 'how', I intend to speak about real things, that is about real forms of human religious experience.

Realism or abstraction?

One of the most disappointing experiences in the life of a theologian is to discover how many things are taken for granted in the Church, which have no connection at all with reality, either historical or personal. If he is not very sincere and honest, he gets used after a time to a world of abstract and almost mythical statements and theories, whose acceptance might eventually witness to his faithfulness towards his Church and her ways of thinking, but not to his intellectual honesty nor his sense of reality. The way we speak, for instance, about 'infallibility' has very often only a tenuous link with historical and factual reality. I don't deny the basic sincerity of the faith of which this attitude may be the expression. But we seem to have this kind of curious tendency in the Western Church to express our existential attitude of faith through various speculative systems or theories, which remain impervious to any serious religious experience. There is almost a schizophrenic mentality of sorts, in which the realities of faith and the humble realities of our human experience belong to two separate worlds. Some even think that the abstract and rational form of those myths, for myths they are, though their structure is conceptional and logical, compensate for the lack of reality. This attitude is very dangerous indeed in an age where our more vital and dynamic Church-members are obsessed by a deep craving for sincerity and authenticity. We are convinced that we touch here one of the deepest reasons why our youth is feeling itself more and more estranged from the Church and her religious language. There is indeed no knowledge or certitude among human beings which is not somewhere connected with personal or corporate experience. And it is a tragic illusion to think that the 'supernatural' as such can dispense and free us from this unavoidable necessity. To take up our example again: nobody can seriously believe in any infallibility if there is no true experience of it somewhere and somehow. And I do not need to say that the simple restatement of the dogmatic truth does not make for any real experience.

It is by no means a valid excuse to plead that God and his saving activity with men is a mystery. It is true that a divine mystery cannot be exhaustively expressed in a rational and conceptual system. But any divine mystery does indeed possess a deep meaning for our personal and corporate religious life, since revelation was never given to feed our intellectual curiosity, but for the achievement of our salvation. We cannot, for instance, elaborate an adequate rational view of the trinitarian mystery, but our faith in the Trinity has no meaning if it does not express itself in our actual life, liturgical, sacramental, spiritual and mystical.

In stressing this view of the truths and realities of our faith, we should remain aware of the fact that this was not a commonly accepted approach of our handbook-theology of the last century. All of us are in need of a radical re-education and theological conversion. For those who feel unable to accept this approach to theology and to theological reflection, which was so common to the Fathers and the great Scholastics, much of what follows will remain meaningless, and even seem dangerous. But I prefer to warn you honestly beforehand, so as to help you to take the proper attitude and to orientate your attention towards the proper perspective from the start.

'Old' and 'new' theology

Another problem is our common need to bridge the gap

between the old and the new theology. Those are very inexact terms, since the new theology finds quite a lot of its inspiration in the older traditions of the patristic and scholastic age: Our so-called 'old theology', which to so many seems safe and sound, is on the contrary, when we care to look at the history of the Church, a rather recent form of theology. This seemingly 'eternal' theology is the result of a rupture in the theological tradition through the predominance of rationalism from the eighteenth century on. This rationalistic impact and perversion explains the deep loss of our mystical and spiritual traditions, which became despised and suspect, and also the distrust of any religious experience, not to speak of the social dimensions of the crisis, when the Church accepted more and more the defensive attitude of a ghetto-Church with its typical sectarian characteristics.

If this is true, and I think it is, then we have the duty to bridge and explain the gap between both those traditions of theology for people who were educated in the so-called old tradition. This is not as easy as it might look. It is not only a question of a new language, or of a different kind of conceptual system, but it is a question of a completely new mentality, of a different insight into the modes of our human approach to reality, and so to truth.[1]

Here lies the deepest reason for so many misunderstandings between honest and sincere members of our Church. The two groups live in quite different worlds. Some are still unable to think in categories different from those we were accustomed to before the last war. Some others are already unable to understan the real religious concern and the ways of thought of the first half of the century. I am convinced that it is the task of those who have lived in both worlds to help in translating one language into the other. This seems to me the most urgent pastoral need of our day.

Revelation before philosophy

But let us return to our topic, the nature of revelation. To introduce you to this new approach to the theology of revelation, I would like to start with an elementary and short philosophical consideration.

We know that philosophy cannot prove the existence of revelation. In a certain sense philosophers have to think as if there was no revelation at all. But a philosopher must be able to answer the following question: let us suppose the existence of a true divine revelation, what kind of activity in God and in human beings is necessarily implied by the acceptance of this fact? What kind of relation between God and man makes this possible? A philosopher has some knowledge of human existence. How can a human being be reached by the eternal and transcendent divinity? One might, however, prefer a better formulation of our problem, especially when thinking of a Christian philosopher. Have you something to say about the meaningfulness of the fact of revelation which you accept as a member of the Christian Church? 'Meaningfulness' is our modern term. The older theology tried the same approach, talking of the 'convenient or congruous aspects' of a mystery. Vatican I expounded this fittingly in nineteenth-century terms: 'Reason, indeed, enlightened by faith, when it seeks earnestly, piously, and calmly, attains by a gift from God some understanding, and that very fruitful, of mysteries; partly from the analogy of those things which it naturally knows, partly from the relations the mysteries bear to one another, and to the last end of man.'[2]

Revelation as a dialogue

The model we traditionally use to explain the mystery of God's divine revealing activity is the dialogue.[3] Revelation is indeed a unique form of communication.

It is first a dialogue which ought to start with God himself. There is unavoidably what we call nowadays a vertical dimension. This is already a decisive point. Some people today seem to be ready to speak of revelation as soon as they meet some kind of human spontaneity, new insight or creativity either poetical, artistical or philosophical. As long as this process remains a purely human, and thus a purely horizontal creative activity of man, it would be fallacious to regard it as a divine revelation, except in a very large and symbolic sense, as, perhaps, when Plato was writing his dialogue about the essence of poetry in *Ion*. By the way, the fact that even Plato accepted the necessity of a kind of initiative from the inner 'daimon' in the process of a poetic inspiration might suggest some deeper philosophical reflection. A divine revelation entails in its true sense a divine initiative in freedom, fully gratuitous, a spontaneous choice to reach human consciousness and life in one way or another. This initiative does not limit itself to a mere prompting of the reflective process in man. It is necessarily a radical dimension which determines the whole process up to its final achievement in huma language and symbolism. It is important to remember this basic statement in order to understand fully what follows about the human aspect of revelation.

From the human side, however, a real revelation cannot remain a purely passive process of absorption of alien knowledge, more or less like the so-called 'innate ideas' theologians sometimes talk about. First, that kind of knowledge does not exist at our level of existence. Every knowledge or spiritual perception is the necessary result of a human activity too, simply because knowledge is radically an activity in itself.

Revelation and language

But there is a still more visible and tangible reason for this, a reason accessible to all, even those not so familiar with philosophical thought. It is clear that any revelation whatsoever has finally to reach expression in human language. If we accept that, as human beings, we are indeed unable to think except in and through a human language, this necessity is seen to be absolute. This principle has to be kept in mind up to the very end of this paper. We cannot accept nowadays the more or less platonizing view of human knowledge, where inner thought and outward language are developed parallel to each other, on two separate levels, as it were. Augustine gives us a good example of this when he thinks that language is a consequence of original sin.[4] We wish to avoid in our theological interpretation of revelation any dualism, even of the latent variety, in the process of knowledge. This will be particularly important when we consider inner experience, as the focal point where revelation occurs concretely.

One can have, of course, the primitive and fundamentalistic

illusion that God himself is talking in one of our languages, that in a miraculous way he is producing that kind of articulated sound which belongs either to Hebrew or to Aramaic or to Greek, and this either in our inner consciousness or outwardly in the air so as to reach the ears of those who are listening. I have a great-aunt, more than ninety years old, a religious sister, who many years ago refused to recognize some fake apparitions of Our Lady of Flanders, because Our Lady seemed to speak Flemish and not the more cultured and 'celestial' French she was expecting. She was right about the apparitions, but the motive for disbelieving was false.

If we don't want to elaborate abstract theories about the nature of revelation again, the very facts of history and experience show us that every divine revealing activity resulted in some spoken language, which manifested clearly the linguistic features of that particular language in that particular time and as spoken by the particular person in question. The language of St Paul is quite different from that of St John and therefore their mediation of God's word too is different. The message of Christ is mediated by Matthew, Mark and Luke, each with variations of language, and different orientations of thought. The language in which God's revelation finally reaches us is doubtless totally human in all its linguistic, literary and structural aspects, though we Christians believe it to be at the same time totally divine, being really the word of God to us. The same could be said of the prophets of the Old Testament. This realistic discovery of modern exegesis is one of the fundamental reasons for the 'uneasiness' of many about the message of the Bible. It shows again how an unrealistic theology always leads towards disaffection and doubt These facts entail the necessity for some active collaboration on the part of those to whom God's revelation is being addressed.[5]

This, however, leads us further to another necessary implication for the human answer to a divine revelation: God never taught us a human language. We received it from our parents and neighbours and the community in the midst of which we were born and grew into adulthood. Language is the ever-developing and living result of a centuries-old tradition and culture. Any language is therefore an already given, man-made texture of thought which is coming to a new life in the very act of revelation. That is why God has indeed to reach us in the very depths of our consciousness and human personality to enable us from the inside, as it were, to understand the divine intention. But God influences us in using the language too, since we understand in and through the spoken word and speak in the very act of understanding.

In other words, for a divine revelation it does not suffice that God starts the movement of reaching out towards us, but this movement influences our talking too. So we see that revelation has necessarily a community dimension, since language belongs intrinsically to the community before we can use it.

Revelation and experience

The important point, already referred to, is that God's activity and initiative is indeed continuous. It has, of course, undoubtedly to reach us from the very inside of our being, where thinking in language and speaking out our thoughts find their source, opening our mind so as to make us capable of perceiving the divine intention. Karl Rahner sometimes expresses it by saying that it is true that God addressed himself in some way to us, but this is only possible if in the movement of reaching out towards us, he at the same time guides us from the very depth of our existence towards him. God's revelation is a question which God addressed to us, a question which at the same time suggests the proper answer.

The fundamental reason for this is that God, as we have seen from the beginning, dwells in unapproachable light. This light is so subtle and violent, so luminous and obscure that our eyes would remain blind to it were it not for the fact that this light creates and prompts in us the right answer, giving us new eyesight and power. To speak to us God has to bring us nearer to him, and therefore to instil in us a kind of divinely supported insight and understanding. This activity of God, by which he brings us towards his deeper understanding, has, as we have seen, a deep personal dimension and at the same time a corporate dimension. Up to now we have especially insisted upon the inner aspect of it. But it is important never to let out of sight the outer corporate and interpersonal aspect.

In short, we can only understand what we feel and experience in ourselves. Experience is the source of all human knowledge. We have no experience of God himself, of his thoughts or understanding. Therefore God cannot speak to us if in the very act of addressing himself to us he is not already speaking in us, and with us, and in a certain sense for us.

St Paul writes in chapter 8 of his epistle to the Romans: 'The Spirit comes to help us in our weakness. For when we cannot choose words in order to pray properly, the Spirit himself expresses our plea in a way that could never be put into words, and God who knows everything in our hearts knows perfectly well what he means, and that the pleas of the saints expressed by the Spirit are according to the mind of God' (*Rom.* 8:26-27) And St John wrote the following profound statement which found in St Augustine one of its most moving commentators: 'No one can come to me unless he is drawn by the Father who sent me, and I will raise him up at the last day. It is written in the prophets: "They will all be taught by God", And to hear the teaching of the Father, and learn from it, is to come to me' (*John* 6:44-45).[6]

Grace and the experience of grace

If this is true, we recognize in this analysis of the divine revealing activity the same model of thought, of interpersonal relations, that we already know from a sound theology of grace.[7] It is therefore our intention when trying to set out in the following pages a theology of divine revelation, to build upon the rich tradition of the theology of grace and of the mystical life, which were a common possession of all schools of theology and spirituality before the tragic rupture in the eighteenth century during the Enlightenment.

This period caused one of the most dramatic losses in our tradition, which is still not fully repaired. Since the Second World War, however, the theology of grace, nowadays more properly expressed in terms of personal relationship, in terms of presence, dialogue and encounter, is becoming again the common possession of western Christendom.

Regarding the spiritual tradition, however, mystical theology is still under a cloud. Many suspect the very word 'mysticism'.

In most cases they don't know what it means. They leave it to contemplative and supposedly world-estranged religious in abbeys and convents. The still common spontaneous reaction is that it is a rather 'dangerous' thing to handle. In brief our mystical tradition is lost. Therefore we simply ignore what it is all about, and leave it to marginal, innocent and harmless people who have nothing better to do.

The later Jesuit theology of grace, the so-called Suarezianism, especially after the eighteenth century under the influence of Cartesianism, went so far as to deny the very possibility of any real inner experience of grace outside the extraordinary cases of 'mystical' charisms. I am personally convinced that this refusal to accept a real spiritual experience of God's living presence in us as the basic situation of every believing man, meant the doom of this kind of theology. Severed from the only source of knowledge we humans have, and from one of the most powerful spiritual traditions in the East as in the West, this kind of theology was condemned to aridity and the endless abstract controversies about predestination and freedom which our former generation of theologians and seminarians received as being *the* Catholic doctrine of grace.

In a certain sense one must say that the richer reality of grace, seen as the mystery of the living and loving presence of God in our life, is indeed the crucial focal point where all the other dogmas of our faith—Trinity, Incarnation, redemption, the Church and the sacraments, eternal life and heaven—become real. The mystery of God's grace is nothing else than the inner aspect of spiritual experience and existence through which those dogmas of faith enter into our life, re-creating it from the very inside while in turn they themselves are made meaningful, real and relevant to us.

The nature of this experience

What is now the nature of this inner experience of grace? God—that is, the Father in the Son and through the power of their Spirit—is really and immediately present in our hearts. This living and loving presence touches us, both in our individual existence, and in our corporate togetherness as a community assembled by God himself.[8] We shall consider later the corporate aspect of grace. Our former theology of grace was too individualistic and narrow. Therefore we reject strenuously the classical distinction between 'grace' which is given to any individual and 'charism' which is given for the sanctification of others. This is a false distinction: the deepest personal grace is always given for the salvation of others too.

This active and creative presence of God in us is *immediate*— that is, God himself, without any created intermediary, is reaching us. Incidentally, we know that the true doctrine of created grace never considers this secondary aspect in the movement of grace as an intermediary, but as the normal implication, fruit and bond in us of God's own direct presence in us. This immediacy of God's presence in us forms indeed the basic aspect of it. It makes our experience of God's presence and attraction, at least at the deepest level of our existence, as such *infallible*. Where God himself is immediately attracting us towards himself, this very inspiration cannot but be infallible and true.

We said, however, that this can only be so at the deepest level of our existence, where our human 'intentionality' is being moved by God himself. The problem is, that we do not possess a clear and distinct intuition of our own depth, of our own 'heart' if we prefer to use the biblical term. It is a rather obscure groping towards God which can become very intense and strong, depending on our acceptance of God's grace in faith, hope and charity, but nevertheless remains quite difficult to express and to describe in sharp, rational terms. That was why the later Suarezianism refused to accept it. But talking about a clear and distinct perception, we are already implying the mediation of language. Our concepts and the words by which they are expressed always go together. We could therefore characterize the tension we have described as inner drive towards translation, towards an expression in words and concepts of the content of this deep attraction of God in us.

The necessary mediation of human language is very important, because finally, wherever the language we use and the concepts this language refers to, become opaque, as it were, and unable to express the divine presence, the experience itself becomes impossible, at least, in the sense that it cannot emerge to a more or less conscious 'expressed' awareness. Since we accept that God's presence is working in every human being who is opening himself to higher and deeper values in full sincerity, we are confronted with a dramatic paradox, which is one of the most important problems of modern atheism. God's grace is working in every human being, but for many atheists, the language and the whole insight into life which is implied by this language excludes God, for whatever reasons—and they are many and complex. So though the source of the experience is really there, it is unable to come through, to emerge properly at the level of human consciousness, because the words and the thoughts they carry have become unsuitable to express it. That is the reason why in full honesty one may contend that the experience of God's presence through his gracious activity is not universal, though from the point of view of God all men are being addressed. One can of course try to find out whether this deeper reality, in atheism for instance, is being expressed in other symbolic ways where God is explicitly excluded, though, at least for those who believe, he is still there.

This paradox confronts us with a problem of intellectual honesty. We have on the one hand to respect people who contend that they do not have any experience of God, which is quite true in the situation in which they are. On the other hand, nobody can prevent us, with great discretion and humility, from recognizing God's loving presence in the values and ideals unbelievers are dying for—that is, every time they commit themselves to absolute values and final goals. Here again we discover the importance, in the whole process of revelation, of human language and symbolism, and of the community in which any particular man is living.

Though our experience of God is doubtless immediate and infallible in its very core, there remains still the very arduous problem of identifying it, a problem that is intimately and unavoidably connected with the language and its accepted meanings as inherited from the community. That is why we said that we have no spontaneous, clear and distinct consciousness of this deeper experience, why we call it, in the technical terms of theology, obscure and indistinct.

It is typical, therefore, that the mystical writers, who had, of course, a richer experience of God's presence than we have, have avoided most of the symbols taken from light and sight, the natural human archetypes of a clear intellectual perception. They prefer to use the symbols taken from the other senses, talking of a spiritual taste, a deeper feeling or awareness, a groping towards the divine reality, a touching of God's presence, as the Venerable Ruysbroeck did, a hearing of the inner word, a smelling of his perfume, or a sweetness. It is indeed not a clear insight, but something analogous to a spiritual *instinct*, a kind of sense for truth and goodness, the 'sensus Dei' that they like to refer to. It is for the same reason that we normally speak of this kind of experience only in symbols and images, and not so easily in notional and conceptula terms. And even the Flemish mystic, John van Ruysbroeck (who is one of the very few who elaborated a philosophy and theology based upon his mystical experience, adopting for this purpose many categories of Denys the Areopagite), very often concludes the exposition of his books with the remark: this can only be understood by people who have experienced the same. And this, as is also the case with the atheists, means that his readers need not only a deep and similar experience, but also familiarity with his language in order to understand what he is saying.

Nor do we experience God's divine presence in its purity; one would almost say in its chemical purity. For we have no clear insight into the depth of our existence, but perceive it only in our freely accepted activity. It is the same with the experience of grace. We cannot perceive it directly, but only in the very activity of our responding to it. The more we open ourselves to the attraction of this presence, the more deeply we experience the inner motion God is initiating in us through his presence. And here is another reason why this description of ours might not be convincing to some people. To perceive it we have indeed to live accordingly, and of course we do need, too, a certain spiritual education and tradition. But this again is connected with the language and the meanings we receive from our contemporaries. Language and whatever a given, concrete language supports is indeed a crystallization of a long human experience in a given culture and history.

We cannot forget that this doctrine, almost always evident during the twelve former centuries in the history of the Church and of theology, was lost in the eighteenth century, and so too were the language and the spiritual tradition which go with it. The words we have to use to explain it have now lost their old meanings; worse, they have acquired distorted meanings, as in the case of whatever is connected with 'mysticism', so that they obscure whatever we try to express.

We cannot partake in any experience of God's presence as we can enjoy together the loveliness of the spring, the charms of poetry and music. The experience of God's living presence—up to now I have purposely avoided using the expression 'the experience of God himself' which would be senseless, at least in this life—is without doubt a real experience, in a certain sense the deepest and the most real experience we have. As such it shows some analogy with other human experiences but it has at the same time a uniqueness, in which it differs from all the others. The basic difference is that any experience of God's presence must necessarily remain an experience that is *given*; I mean an experience which remains essentially a *gift*. For as soon as we think that we are bringing God into our possession, where we can manipulate him or his grace, we inevitably destroy the experience itself, making it impossible. God is not to be manipulated or possessed though unhappily that is what many people think mysticism means.

The experience of God's presence is necessarily an experience of something continuously given, offered, freely proposed. From this we infer another essential aspect of this experience. It cannot come to life if we, on our side, do not respond to it in faith, hope and charity, or in whatever form a human being freely and finally accepts 'the other' as the absolute meaning of his life.

But finally it cannot emerge into some awareness and perception without the mediation of language, which means that the full expansion of this experience depends unavoidably upon the experiences of others, upon the way the community has already tried to express this many-faced and endlessly varied experience—

for God addresses himself to all of us in our own individual situations—in a more or less common language and doctrine, namely a certain amount of meanings left at our disposal and for our use to continue and implement the experience of former times. Continually we see how the whole problem of the experience of God's presence possess both a vertical and a truly horizontal and historical dimension. We are as unable to separate one from the other, as we are unable to separate soul and body in a living human being.

But let us once again return to the deep and initial infallibility of this experience, so as to discover why this infallibility is at the same time threatened and obscured. Our experience of God must be infallible in its original depth and reality. But as soon as we try to express it to ourselves and to others in terms of ordinary language, we are confronted with all kind of dangers and obstacles. We have already given the example of many atheists, but it is the fate of us all. The whole process of interpretation is open to error and illusion. This happens because of the various interfering influences of education, heredity, psychology, language and the culture and doctrine stored in it, but especially because of one's sinfulness. The latter is the only radical menace to the purity of our interpretation, because it impairs the very roots of the experience itself. Evil is essentially the refusal of God's attraction and love. This refusal makes it more difficult to perceive just what it is we are refusing.

A 'corporate' experience

At this point we shall turn our attention to the corporate aspect of this experience of grace to which we have already alluded. Before God we stand together. Before God we are but one family. This is true, even for the mystery of grace. It is in our togetherness that this living presence of God manifests itself. Fr Piet Schoonenberg wrote a few years ago: 'In the mystery of grace God has given us to one another.' It seems that God normally uses our interpersonal relations to bring about his own divine presence. We are touching the deepest meaning of the existence of the Church, as a sing, a living symbol, and a mediating community for the redemption of all men.[9]

What do we now mean by 'corporate experience' of God's presence and activity? The experience of God's presence can only reach us in the depths of our 'heart'. There is no common 'personality' behind our individuality. 'Corporate experience' has another meaning; it reminds us of the necessary horizontal dimension of our experience. We are, as we have already seen, each of us incapable of expressing and translating for ourselves and for others the deeper content, the meaning and the orientation of the divine inner activity, without some form of language. In this context by the word 'language' we mean whatever instruments of interpersonal communication human beings have at their disposal. And communication includes expression.

We are indeed deeply *dependent* on one another, on our common past and the fullness of experience this past has enshrined for us in the many forms of inherited patterns of thought and behaviour which constitute what we call a culture. This treasure of the Church is to be found in her prayers, liturgy, rituals, dogmatic statements, theological doctrines, ways of life and structures of community; in brief, in her religious culture.

Our deeply personal experience becomes a corporate experience for two reasons. Firstly, the many symbolic forms of treasured former experiences make it possible for me to reach, through the mirror of the language, a real awareness of what has happened to me. Secondly, my personal experience in turn enriches, deepens and develops, again in and through my expression of it, the common treasure of the Church. It is clear that a rich tradition of spirituality fosters a deeper experience for all of us who want to enter into it. But the more intense experience of saints, known or unknown, deepens, strengthens and develops the ecclesial tradition. One may say that the personal experience expands and matures in the climate of a rich religious culture, which in its turn is enriched by the personal experience. From this, we can understand the deep tragedy for the Church when this tradition was lost under the scorn and suspicion of rationalism and juridicism, and by the refusal to acknowledge the validity of a real, though often weak and obscure, experience of God's presence, which is the *normal* condition of the 'state of grace' and the life of faith.

The corporate dimension of this experience of grace has another aspect, which sheds a new light upon the deeper nature of the Church as a 'communion of faith', and at the same time upon the deeper nature of her 'infallibility'. First, from a more general experience of human existence we see that all humanity today is slowly discovering truth together, that it is establishing the possibility of freedom and love together, creating those 'patterns of behaviour and thought' which make this possible. This togetherness means that we need one another to discover the truth about ourselves, to build up those conditions of life which foster the expansion of human dignity and freedom.

The same is true of our experience of God in grace. In the communion of faith and charity the truth which Christ entrusted to his Church is being treasured, deepened and developed. Indeed, within the Church the dialogue in its many forms gives us a guarantee that the corporate experience of the Church retains its original authenticity in its continuous evolution and development throughout history. Staying together, and so being faithful to Christ, we are enabled to avoid errors and illusions, which threaten the very experience by which we live.

The older theology said that no individual revelation that was against the faith could be accepted by the Church. But what is the real meaning of this, if we refuse to reduce the Church to juridical relations of authority and blind obedience? It means that every personal experience of God's grace is necessarily to be confronted with the language of faith and with the actual doctrine of the living Church. There is no Church up in the air, as a platonic hypostasis. *We* are the Church. The Church is the community of the many, interrelated by faith, worship and ways of life.

When we now finally remember that the whole process of experiencing God's presence remains inevitably under the primacy of God's initiative and moving love, we see much better why God brought us together in the Church, as a means of salvation. Through and in the Church God is bringing us nearer to himself, opening us up to his attraction and inspiration, preserving us in the obedience of faith. Holding us within the Church he is at the same time disposing us to meet him in the depth of our 'hearts'.

Revelation as a form of experience

Up to now we have described some aspects of a theology of grace from the point of view of the tradition concerning our experience of grace, and of the presence of God in it. Many more things could be said about this,[10] but we have to keep to our subject, the nature of revelation. Our intention here is to explain the process of revelation, as one of the most important aspects of the very movement of God's gracious presence in us, and for this reason, we have devoted considerable space to the theology of the experience of grace.

Looking at the history of the origin and growth of the books of the Bible, which are one of the most important expressions of God's revelation, we see that there was never any revelation out of the blue, so to speak, falling out of the sky as a meteorite— that is, in an abstract and doctrinaire way without any connection with the situation in which the prophets or the apostles concerned found themselves. Even the vision of God by Isaiah (*Is.* 6) explains the reason and the source of his mission as a prophet.

Revelation is always given *about* something the man receiving God's revelation sees, knows, meets, suffers or enjoys. For the prophets, for instance, it was the terrible crisis of Israel after the glory of king Solomon, the division into two kingdoms, the attacks from without, the religious confusion within, the exile and the dispersion, and the final return to Jerusalem. For the apostles it was the life of the primitive Church with its local and more universal problems, the incipient heresies, the divisions and strifes, the moral problems in a pagan world, and so on. God is not a schoolmaster, teaching his schoolboys things which are quite unconnected with their daily life. Revelation always gives us some deeper insight into what we already know, helping us to look *behind* the external appearances and impressions. Revelation gives us an insight into the real meaning or value of what we are confronted with in our day-to-day life or in the life of the community and the people.

This is quite evident whenever we study the origin and the background of most of the prophetic books of the Old Testament which contain the core of the divine message in the Old Covenant.

It is the same with the epistles of the apostles in the New Testament. There is no systematic or theoretical doctrine, but a continuous interpretation of the meaning of Christian life in the various situations in which the primitive Church found herself. One of the most difficult points in the interpretation of the doctrine of the apostles is that they assimilated the teaching of Christ with a very special bias, the conviction that the end of the world was near. Some statements of St Paul cannot be understood, for instance those about marriage, if we don't take this particular situation of the apostolic Church into account.

It is more difficult to reconstruct the actual form of the preaching of Christ, since the gospels are a redactionally worked up survey, with a catechetical intent, of what Christ did and said. In the gospels, too, the conviction of the proximate return of the Lord seasoned the final redaction of his teachings. And we also have to reckon with the fact that as historians, the authors, while neither ignoring nor neglecting the facts, were especially interested in indicating their deeper meaning. This is a well-known approach of all eastern writers either profane or religious. But this oriental attitude played a special role in treasuring for our benefit the deeper meaning of those facts as a real form of 'revelation. from God.

Nevertheless there is no doubt Christ preached to the Jews and to his disciples in a very concrete way. His teaching was neither systematic nor abstract. His concern was the inner conversion of the soul, because the kingdom of God was nigh. His whole effort tended to explain the decisive meaning of his coming and the significance of his future death and resurrection at that moment of history. Incidentally that is the reason why most of the original symbols of faith are about facts and their meaning for our life, and not about dogmas or theories. The definition of dogmas followed later in the confrontation of the Church with heretical movements.

We know that along with the Bible the living tradition of the Church is also instrumental in the transmission of the content of revelation. But what is the tradition of the Church if not her daily and corporate life of faith? Vatican II gives a good description of tradition: 'Now what was handed on by the apostles includes everything which contributes to the holiness of life, and the increase in faith of the People of God; and so the Church, in her teaching, life and worship, perpetuates and hands on to all generations all that she herself is, all that she believes.'[11]

After this brief survey of the different ways that revelation has come to us, with their essential characteristics, we may safely return to the concrete form of revelation which supports our Christian faith. This revelation, which slowly ripened inside the community of the Old Covenant, through many crises indeed, in the course of history which lasted almost ten centuries, was perfected and accomplished in Christ and the apostolic Church.

We leave out for the moment the role of Christ, for, being unique and supreme, it seems impossible to start with him, if we want to understand the human structures God used in his revelation. Not possessing Christ's unique relationship and intimacy with his Father, we have in our experience no real point of comparison with the psychology of Christ's knowledge, except, from a great distance, in some of the highest points in the mystical tradition. The prophets, the saints and the apostles, on the contrary, were men as we are. We have in common with them the experience of mystical life and of an intense life of grace. It is therefore easier to start with them, though we know that their mediation without that of Christ is meaningless and void.

Revelation, we have said, is but one of the most important aspects of the experience of grace as an experience of God's living and loving presence in us, either individually or corporately.

This creative and active presence of God causes, in one who is opening himself to God's motion[12] in the very core of his being, an inner attraction and inclination towards God, his truth, his goodness and reality. This attraction is direct and immediate, and therefore basically infallible. We have already seen that this inner attraction, inclination and motion—the three different terms well-known to theologians—give us a deep and sure instinct of what God is, or better, of the direction in which we have to look and reach for God, of the whole orientation that our being, our mind and freedom ought to receive on our journey towards God. This inner instinct and spiritual taste enables us to detect, to recognize and to identify among the many things, situations and possible activities we are confronted with in our life, among the many opinions, teachings and traditions, doctrines and more general views we hear about, among the bewildering variety of values human society has elaborated and is fighting for—to recognize and to identify those truths and values which smell, I would say, or which bear the seal of God, those values and insights which we feel are leading us towards God, especially the deeper meaning of whatever is happening to us, as the blurred image and mirror of God's remote and yet very close presence. 'Now we are seeing a dim reflection in a mirror; but then we shall be seeing face to face' (1 *Cor.* 13:12). It is as the light of the evening sun which colours the gold and the silver with strange shades of brilliance, leaving the dirt in darkness.

This process of sifting and identification takes time in the life of man. The whole presupposition of this interpretation is the deep conviction that we do not possess the truth in faith, but that the truth possesses us, and secondly, that this discovery of God's truth requires the whole history of men. That is the reason why Vatican II called the Church the *pilgrim* Church. Here on earth we are essentially on our way, on our way towards God who is to be met in Christ by the power of his Spirit. It is a process which matures in a religious community, in the communion and the dialogue of faith. For, as we have seen before, this process is not to be separated from its necessary complement, the evolution of human language and symbols, prompted by this experience and in its turn promoting it because a richer language makes for a deeper experience.

It is a unique spiritual venture which is daily enriched by experience and prayer. Out of this slow process of maturation into consciousness grows a fundamental option and reorientation or conversion of our whole life, leading to an ever deeper certitude and greater freedom. It expresses itself spontaneously in the various forms of life and faith, in liturgy and rite, in prayer and hymns, in moral behaviour and interpersonal communication, and finally it finds expression in writings.

This inner attraction of God's grace, the inward prompting of the Holy Spirit, moves the whole body of the faithful. That is very important, for it gives the necessary human, cultural and religious foundation upon which the more intense forms of revelation can be based. For this same movement of grace acquires a greater intensity and quality with those men of God, prophets, saints or apostles whom God chooses and sends to his people. This interaction between the whole community and the guidance of the chosen men of God is again a normal structure in the discovery of truth and values which God respects and uses, as he always respects the nature of his own creatures, even in the so-called 'supernatural' order! This functional structure of the People of God is the basis for the communion of faith and the well-known but still practically ignored collegiality inside the ministry.

Objections

Those are the fundamental points I wanted to stress in relation to a better interpretation of the process of revelation. They convince me. But to convince you, I am sure, many objections have first to be answered. That this process of a spiritual experience is authentic, I think everybody knows who is familiar with our spiritual tradition. But the question is whether that process can be called 'revelation'. That is the point we still have to tackle.

In other words we seem to confuse the unique reality of 'revelation' with an immense variety and scale of spiritual phenomena in our life of faith, which seem to have nothing to do with 'revelation' as such. Or more technically, universally accepted distinctions in theology are simply disregarded.

We neglect first the distinction between the uniqueness of God's revelation in Christ and the broader and rather vague trends of religious experience in other religions, outside Christianity. We neglect or ignore secondly the point which was re-discovered at Vatican II, the distinction between the basic act of God in revelation and its instrumental transmission through the mediation of Scriptures and the tradition of the Church.[13] Thirdly, classical theology teaches that there is no more revelation in the Church after the death of the last apostle—that is, of St John, I presume. The apostolic Church furnished the time, the space and the place for the final 'public revelation' of God, as Vatican II writes;[14] after that tradition consists essentially in handing on the unchanged truth. These are quite clear distinctions which simply appear to have vanished in our interpretation of the process of revelation.

Finally, we seem to neglect the differences between the real process of revelation and the ordinary life of faith under the influence of divine graces. Does every inner experience become a 'revelation'? Nobody ever dared to pretend this! But there is still probably a more radical and crucial objection. Are we right when we understand this kind of inner experience, albeit under the evident influence of God's grace, as the true and saving word of God to his Church, and so to the whole world?

First I agree as a whole with the general trend of the objections that the former clear-cut distinctions of classical theology have indeed become smudged and blurred or at least watered down so as to seem to threaten the uniqueness of revelation itself. We seem to be left with an interpretation that is so vague and so confusing that, fitting everything, in the end it fits nothing. We Roman Catholics, especially under the influence of the Cartesianism and rationalism still latent in our theology, may continue to expect 'clear and distinct ideas' from our theologians. The real question is whether life is as 'clear and distinct' as we dream it to be. But the best answer is to take the objections I have mentioned and to deal with them one by one.

In our view there is apparently no real difference between the notion of the revelation in Christ and the general religious experience in other religions. The whole question boils down to whether we have to refuse, out of fidelity to our faith, the possibility of an initial revelation, and even of a continuous form of revelation outside Christianity. Our handbook-theology probably has no doubt about a negative answer. The negative answer was certainly common in the last centuries, after the tragic controversies about the Far-Eastern rites.[15] This answer, however, is not self-evident. There is a very interesting tradition among the Church Fathers of the first seven centuries which acknowledges a certain initial revelation in the Greek and Roman religions, or in the religions before the patriarchs. One of the most striking witnesses to this tradition is St Augustine. I have written elsewhere about this, and quoted important studies dealing with this theme. One of the most striking articles is that of Fr Yves Congar with the title 'Ecclesia ab Abel', a common theme among the Fathers.[16]

Quite recently Karl Rahner has simply reversed the objection. Once we accept that the revelation which has indeed a unique and exclusive role in Christianity, is nevertheless not absent from religious experience outside Christianity, even among atheists, then we understand for the first time the unique role of the Church as consisting in that *ministry* to the whole world which Vatican II has so strongly emphasized. She has indeed to bring to light and to full expression and life what is already there. This makes, he writes, for a more radical and a clearer understanding of what Christianity really is.[17]

We are thus perfectly justified, when in our interpretation of the process of revelation in Christianity and the non-Christian religions, we accept only a difference in quality and intensity, exclusively based on the uniqueness of Christ, but not a difference in nature.

Secondly, have we not neglected the necessary distinction between between God himself as the source of revelation, and the means of transmission, which are the Scriptures and the tradition of the Church?

Let us start with tradition, for historically, it comes before the Scriptures, and besides, it seems easier to tackle than the Scriptures.

The common theological view in our Church is quite clear. Christ entrusted the primitive Church with the fullness of truth. After the death of Christ the Church had nothing else to do except to keep this treasure alive, intact and inviolate. That would be quite clear, indeed, if the entrusted treasure had been a sum of money, a building, or even a holy book, written by Christ himself for instance. But this treasure is a completely new way of life, and this in an ever-changing world!

Therefore even classical theology was forced to add a few more specifications. Because of the very complex evolution of life in the primitive Church it was said that revelation ended, not with the death or the ascension of Christ, which logically would be expected, but with the death of the last apostle which, however, is not so meaningful any more, especially since we know or at least suspect that some books of the New Testament were written after the death of St John.

The nineteenth century, especially with J. A. Moehler in Tübingen and J. H. Newman in England, added the notion of the development of dogma as a further qualification of the nature of the Church's tradition. After a few useless attempts on the part of scholastic theology to restrict the development of dogma to purely external aspects or to a mere logical and conceptual expansion from the implicit towards the explicit formulation of dogma, or from the virtual to the formal expression of it, we are now discovering a reality of evolution, which is at least richer, more complex and involved than we had previously thought. Our knowledge and sense of history is now sharper. We are unearthing the dimensions of time, even in the texture of our thoughts. Probably we are now making a real effort towards a greater sincerity and intellectual honesty in relation to the historical facts we too easily manipulated before.

So nowadays the sharp frontier-line between revelation and emerging and continuing tradition is blurred. It seems that we are forced to look for a more radical and intrinsic reason for the difference between revelation and pure tradition than the too external and temporal delimitations, which it seems to me were not totally free from a juridical bias.

I think there is one radical and intrinsic specification we all know but to my mind keep too much in the background of our thoughts. There is in the relation between the God of our salvation and humanity one central and unique point in history, namely the unique role of Christ. From this fundamental approach revelation is primarily and formally connected with the event of Christ, with his words and acts, and with the immediate witnesses of his coming. Christ did not come into a vacuum, but was sent to a community, the people of Israel. Revelation being the word of God to a particular group of men, the whole dialectical process has to be retained as *one* dialogical reality which is indeed the primary event of God's revelation. Other subsequent delimita-

tions in time or space are ineffective. Revelation is an interpersonal reality, a fact of communication. It can only be rightly
and sufficiently described when we look at the persons who took
part in this primary event. In this sense indeed there is 'no further
public revelation before the glorious manifestation of Our Lord
Jesus Christ' as Vatican II very wisely states.[18]

To understand this role of Christ some will have to correct
their notion of revelation. Up to Vatican II there were not a
few theologians who insisted upon the necessity of limiting the
nature of revelation to a particular divine way of communicating
to men a certain number of new *notions* about God and his
saving relation to men. Against strong opposition Vatican II
broadened this still unconciously rationalistic definition of
revelation, saying: 'This commission [of handing on the revelation
of Christ] was faithfully fulfilled by the apostles who, by their
oral preaching, by example, and by ordinances, handed on what
they had received from the lips of Christ, from living with him,
and from what he did, or what they had learned through the
prompting of the Holy Spirit. The commission was fulfilled too,
by those apostles and apostolic men who under the inspiration
of the same Holy Spirit committed the message of salvation to
writing.'[19]

We see how the Council itself not only refers to the verbal
teachings of Christ, but to his life, example and activity. At the
same time, adding the 'promptings of the Holy Spirit' formally
as an 'inspiration' in writing the books of the New Testament,
the Council—as we did, though in a more limited way—integrated
the inner guidance and motion of the Spirit into the whole process
of revelation.

This uniqueness of Christ is, of course, decisive in understanding the nature of revelation in its primary and most intensive
function. We have, however, to connect it with the Church, first
symbolically realized in the 'Remnant', the Twelve. But even
after the Twelve the Church remains Christ's visibility on earth,
his body existing not for her own sake, but, in imitation of her
Lord, for the salvation of the world.

If this is true we possess a richer and more real notion of
revelation; a new way of life before God is given gratuitously

through the saving activity of Christ and his Spirit. That is the treasure which has been entrusted to the Church. This new life is a thoroughly gracious gift of the Father in his Son through the inner motion of the Spirit who proceeds from both. It supports at the same time the inward cohesive texture of the new community and its outward manifestation in words and deeds. As there is necessarily a soul and a body in the unity of the human person, there is in the Church an inner power and motion of grace and an outward preaching and behaviour of the apostles and the disciples. We are re-discovering from a different and more dogmatic perspective the unity of the vertical and the horizontal or corporate dimensions of revelation.

From this it appears clearly that the tradition of the Church is not radically different from the divine activity of revelation. There are, however, two very important differences which force us to make a distinction between them. No one after the death of Christ possesses the same universal authority as he himself possessed in his own right. Secondly, no one has known the same intimacy and immediacy with Christ as the apostles and the first contemporaries of Christ, the chosen witnesses of his life, death and resurrection. Therefore, not even a pope, an episcopate, an ecumenical council or a saint with a very deep mystical intimacy with God, can partake in this universal commission and mission. Medieval theology never denied the possibility of a particular revelation, but outside the living unity of Christ with the apostolic Church, no particular revelation might obtain universal authority.

Without doubt God's saving activity, at least at the level of the divine influx of God's presence in the motion of grace, is fundamentally the same everywhere and in all times. Nothing on earth is capable of limiting God's universal love and initiative. And that is the reality by which all these ecclesial and extra-ecclesial realities we are discussing as well as others we are not referring to, as for instance the whole sacramental life, are intimately and really connected.[20]

But God saves us as human beings, for whom interpersonal relations form the very texture of our corporate existence. This corporate dimension of human existence implies at the same time the dimension of historicity, and this now, in its turn, involves the special role of the 'beginning' as a function of any further evolution. This 'beginning' starts fundamentally with the living Christ. The coming of Christ was intended for the whole world. It is of the nature of the human condition that this world cannot be reached except in and through the mediation of a community in time and place. So we must necessarily see the coming of the Lord together with his messianic community of the founding Church as the central event of our salvation. And therefore revelation in the strict sense can only be accepted within this very event of universal salvation.

Against this historical and dogmatic background we might now try to understand the unique role of the Scriptures. Historically the Scriptures are one of the first crystallizations of emerging tradition since they are nothing other than the written 'expression' of the unique event which is central to that tradition.

On the other hand Scripture, at least according to not a few theologians, does have an authority and a real precedence over the Church's later tradition, especially after the apostolic Church, because this Church was the founding Church, the Church of the beginning, partaking in the universal mission of her Lord, and therefore the documents belonging to this Church retain a binding authority for later times. The Scriptures are the so-called *norma normans* of our Church, the 'binding norm' of our faith throughout all times, peoples and nations.

But we believe something more. We confess that the Scripture, though doubtless the work of men, is at the same time the word of God to us. Reading the Bible we hear God addressing to us the same words spoken by the prophet Nathan to David after his sin: 'You are the man' (2 *Sam.* 12:7). You are the man for whom this was written! In former times the interpretations of the nature of inspiration might have stressed the part played by God, or on the contrary the part played by the sacred author. In recent years there has been a clear tendency to approach an understanding of inspiration from a less individualistic standpoint, not as if the fact of inspiration regarded only God, the Spirit and the sacred writer himself without any relation to the community in which and for whom he was writing. We have seen that this narrow perspective is false, philosophically and theologically as well. The exegetes were brought to the new perspective by a better knowledge of the origin and the development of the sacred books.

The Bible is indeed the word of God to us, to the Church and to every member of the Church, transmitting the words of Christ, his message. This message is undoubtedly the principal content of the Bible, and of its truth. Vatican II expresses this clearly, being even specific than most theologians would have dared to be before the Council. 'Therefore, since everything asserted by the inspired authors or sacred writers must be held to be asserted by the Holy Spirit, it follows that the books of Scripture must be acknowledged as teaching firmly, faithfully and without error *that* truth which God wanted put into the sacred writings *for the sake of our salvation*'.[21]

In our theological tradition 'inspiration' is different from 'revelation'. Inspiration effects two things. Firstly, this text is in a particular sense the word of God. Thus the books of the Bible contain God's revelation. Secondly, as a consequence, they cannot lead us into error in what they state as belonging to God's revelation, in contrast with what they simply refer to or imply, as for example, some time-bound cultural, scientific or philosophical views. The sacred books therefore mediate to us the content of God's revelation. They belong to that kind of activity we have analysed before—that is, the human endeavour to express in human words and language the reality of God's saving activity. This human effort is made under the influence of God's Spirit.

I see no difficulty in applying what I said earlier about the whole process of revelation to the more particular process of inspiration with one important exception. In the case of inspiration the inner guidance of the Holy Spirit is formally helping the author in the written formulation of his thought towards an authentic expression of Christian life in the very concrete and ever-changing situation of composing a letter, a story, a catechetical instruction or 'didascalia', a prophecy or an apocalyptic book.

When we consider that modern theology refuses to limit the 'mechanics' of inspiration to any particular author, but wants to integrate into the whole process the collaboration of the community, we see again how the border-line between revelation and inspiration as an active process is fading, though not disappearing. Further it remains a decisive fact that this very community is a 'privileged' community, being the Church of the Beginning, the Church in which the event of Christ took place.

We have now to deal with a more radical objection. Are we really honestly allowed to call that form of individual and corporate spiritual experience which we analysed in the first part of this paper, even when it is based upon the direct and immediate guidance of the Holy Spirit, a true revelation of God? Revelation is indeed, in its original and authentic sense, a powerful, unique notion; better still, a reality which, if true, has a radically decisive meaning for our lives. We are not allowed to play around with it!

My first answer is rather a negative one. I see no other true and meaningful way to explain the process of revelation. I refuse to accept that it is an unavoidable feature of religion that it must make statements and uphold views that nobody can understand. This would be to revert to a nominalistic theology, which explained everything by divine decrees coming down from high heaven. That is too easy, and is no theology at all.

It is necessary to say that revelation is a relational notion. It is doubtless addressed to man and has to be assimilated by him, as he was created by God. Man is a being who discovers the truth about himself and the world he is living in through a lifelong, slow, painful and arduous effort of personal reflection and mutual confrontation with his fellowmen in the concrete community in which he lives. I don't think that God ignored this in his revelation. The other approach to the 'supernatural' realities in our life brings about a dangerous schizophrenia, separating God's activity from the so-called 'natural' realities of creation. God only wanted to lead us further, to manifest some deeper realities of life, to bring us a greater certitude, and to change our life accordingly. Again the primordial goal of revelation is not to feed our curiosity about a kind of unknown and celestial reality; but to bring about our conversion to the true God. God's revelation saves before being instructive, and it only instructs us in order to save us more efficaciously.

Being corporeal, man cannot attain any insight about himself and the world without the language and 'patterns of behaviour' which his own community has built up over so many centuries. Those 'patterns of behaviour' are important, for they are to our freedom and love what language is to our mind.[22] But this language and those 'patterns of behaviour' can only be activated under the drive of one's personal experience. We have even seen that personal experience in its turn is intrinsically dependent on language and the 'patterns of behaviour' so that it may emerge into consciousness and be expressed in ethical and religious activities. The only relation a human being has with the outside reality, whatever it is, comes to life in his own consciousness, in which is reflected continuously, as in a kind of mirror, the content of his encounter with the outside reality.

If God wants to direct his eternal word to this very particular weak, blind and sinful man, there is no other possible way for him than to enter into the intimacy of man's consciousness, kindling and evoking a deeper experience which colours, vivifies and illuminates the many other things he knows. But since this deeper experience remains unexpressed without the aid of his fellowmen, who share with him the language and the ways of life, he needs to reach this deeper self-understanding, God's revelation has inevitably a corporate dimension, the communion of faith of the community.

That this influence of grace, this inner illumination and motion is a true revelation of God we have seen. Without this very motion of the Spirit in man himself and in his fellowmen, the deepened and intensified experience of God's presence and guidance remains impossible. We have already stressed the necessity of God's initiative supporting the whole process.

To be honest, we cannot prove this last statement by direct experience, for we have no experience of any human existence outside the economy of grace. According to an older theological position (which has been revived in recent times) all men live in the so-called 'supernatural order'. This means that all of us are indeed under the influence of God's creative presence, at least under the form of a continuous invitation to accept it, the famous *vorgegebene Gnade*, the offered grace, defended by Karl Rahner.

Nevertheless, I think we are able to perceive indirectly the impossibility of reaching this 'sense of faith' without the motion of the Spirit. In order to experience how much the presence of a loved person means it is not necessary to ask her to leave us for a while. One of the most decisive ways of discovering the meaning and the value of her presence is to enjoy it. This is the more true of an authentic religious experience, where the gratuitousness and the divine enter into the very fabric and texture of the experience itself. This is precisely one of the signs of its authenticity, that it is continuously 'given' to us, and that we perceive it as being continuously given.

The second reason why this inner motion and attraction of God constitutes the structure of God's revelation, is that this active and creative presence remains always under the initiative of God himself. God not only starts the dialogue; he retains the initiative up to the very end—that is, to the communitarian expression of the divine motion in language and life. In view of this, the notion of dialogue could cause some confusion. I have used it because it is esentially a relational notion, imploying the use of liberty and love. With God there is, however, no dialogue in the sense that both parties retain their own full initiative, as is the basic view of pelagianism. Nevertheless in the movement of grace there is a reciprocal relation in so far as man has to answer freely and truly the invitation of God.

Finally this divine initiative is not a kind of neutral power-source, as for instance electricity which shines equally for the poor and the rich. This initiative is born with the living God, a personal God, who looks at us in a personal way. He indeed chooses his prophets and apostles. He guides his sacred writers. He illuminates and inspires his saints. God's free election and primacy bring to this initiative his own, I would almost say, individuality. It is, in a word *par excellence* a personal guidance, reaching every one of us in our concrete situation. Nobody is so concrete as God. Abstraction, as we know, is a typical human weakness!

Conclusion

Our conclusion shall be brief. My only intention has been to show how some modern theologians try to approach many of the well-known themes of dogmatic theology relevant to our own. The kind of theological approach I have adopted is called by Rahner, Schillebeeckx and others the anthropological approach.[23] Among others who have tried the same method in the matter of interpretation of the nature of revelation I would Abbé P. Touilleux, who unhappily presents rather a confusing mixture of scholastic and Husserlian categories.[24] There is an American, Brother Gabriel Moran, from New York.[25] Quite recently a colleague of mine, Fr Louis Monden, published a book in the same vein.[26]

I have followed the same idea, but in my own way, starting from the theology of grace and of the experience of grace. This attempt has no authority other than my own, though I hope the inner coherence may convince others too. In any case I offer this paper to my fellow-theologians and fellow-believers, for I am really convinced of the necessity of a dialogue with others in order to rethink theology. Nobody does it on his own. I have not so much been endeavouring to separate and delimit the so-called 'substance' of our faith in the fact of revelation. That is another topic. Taking the common doctrine inside the Christian Churches for granted, I have simply tried to look for a meaningful interpretation.

I am convinced that this anthropological approach to theology has indeed its own value in our days. First it brings the dogmas nearer to our personal experience. Secondly it shows how the dogmas of our faith have a meaning for our daily life, and how we may be able to reveal this meaning.

This work seems to me particularly important for the interpretation of the process of revelation. Our actual life of faith under the influence of God's presence and grace follows basically the same pattern we have discovered in the process of revelation. Faith means accepting the revealing word of God as source of our life in the same way as the saints, the prophets and the apostles did. Faith is the point of impact where God's word in us fosters a new life. To understand fully and truly the riches of

God's revealing word, we in our turn must follow the same way and tread the same footprints as the apostles did when they heard about God and his saving activity. It is only when we are actually listening to the word of God as the prophets and the saints originally did, that we shall understand God's word in truth, and live accordingly. Otherwise faith remains a curious collection of abstract and rather meaningless statements which we simply store in our mind. But that is not what the word of God is for. St John concludes his gospel with these words: 'These are recorded so that you may believe that Jesus is the Christ, the Son of God, and that believing this you may have life through his name' (*John* 20:31).

Christian Faith as Personal Response

JAMES P. MACKEY

OUR topic has now been suitably placed. Cardinal Koenig has painted the background of contemporary culture against which any present understanding of our topic must be construed and Piet Fransen has filled in the foreground detail, a theology of revelation upon which alone a well-founded concept of faith can be set. It is time now to tackle the central topic itself. The type and structure of the concept of faith which I am expected to paint into the picture is already only too well indicated for me by the very title that was given this talk. Titles, however, are not always decisive, especially when they precede the writing of a paper, and we shall have some critical remarks to address to the title itself.

Solemn pronouncements of the Church

Let us resist the temptation to play the 'It was said to you of old . . . but I say to you' game. This is a game which all young theologians are tempted to play and none has ever entirely resisted. In this case the game would read: it was said to you of old that faith was an intellectual assent to a set of revealed truths . . . but I say to you that faith is an existential commitment, a life lived, a personal response—or whatever.[1] Only those whose enthusiasm for the letter of conciliar definitions renders them oblivious to the spirit and context in which these were issued would be tempted to accuse councils like Trent and Vatican I of proposing an over intellectualized concept of faith. Trent was combating what it believed to be a reduction, on the Reformers' part, of the whole process of man's justification before God to faith alone and a consequent identification of this kind of faith with a kind of trust (*fiducia*) in the divine mercy.[2] Consequently, the Council listed a complex number of steps—for instance, impulsion by divine grace, hope, trust, love, interior renewal, by which the process of justification is achieved; and amongst these it spoke of faith which, it said, is conceived in a man *ex auditu* (*Rom.* 10:17). When this faith is conceived in a man, he moves freely towards God, believing those things to be true which were divinely revealed and promised.[3] Justification, not specifically faith, was the immediate and concrete object of concern of the Council. The Reformers had definitions of faith, too, other than that which they used when trying to isolate very particularly that element by which man is justified before God, e.g. dogmatic-historical faith: the faith which works miracles.

It would be unjust to the Reformers to maintain that their objections to the merit theology in the Roman theory of salvation were wide of the mark. Their attempt to bring to the fore an aspect of the concept of faith which had been more than a little overshadowed by merit theories, precisely the ascept of trust in the saving act of God, got less credit than it deserved. But it would be equally unjust to Trent to insist that here the Council Fathers were setting out to provide us with an adequate theology of faith, and on these terms, to expand on its shortcomings.

It is true that the constitution from the Third Session of Vatican I is entitled *Constitutio de fide Catholica* and that chapter 3 of that constitution is entitled simply 'De Fide'. Nevertheless it is necessary here also to take into account the spirit and the context of the constitution. It is clear that the immediate and concrete object of attention for the participants at Vatican I was not, once again, faith itself, to be treated calmly and exhuastively, but rather the relationships between faith and reason, which had to be dealt with in the unquiet context of a riot of conflicting views. The Hegelian system, the springtide of the European rationalist movement, had submerged the traditional faith in the concepts of human reason. Traditional doctrines such as Trinity and Incarnation became 'intellectual symbols' or 'imperfect concepts', useful, even necessary as such, yes, but the true content of which could be expressed better in the perfect concepts of Hegelian philosophy.

Faced with such monopolizing movement of human reason it was all too tempting for some, who wished to say that special divine revelation had something extra to offer over and above what such exercise of human reason could accomplish, to declare this extra to be non-rational, absurd, almost in the sense of irrational. To many this is the impression which that stalwart defender of Christianity in the rationalist age, Kierkegaard, conveyed.

On the Roman Catholic side there were those like Hermes and Gunther who were officially condemned for taking over into their thought too much of the rationalist spirit. They were therefore suspected of diluting the faith. On the other hand, there were the fideists and traditionalists (Bautain); De Bonald, De Maistre, Bonnetty). Fideism and traditionalism both reacted against the predominantly rationalist movement of European philosophy. Reacting against Descartes' methodic doubt, against the rationalism that developed from his system, against all the evils[8]they saw stemming from this—the so-called enlightenment, the agnostic and atheistic encyclopedists, the French Revolution, the spread of unrest and unbelief—these movements turned hostile, not simply to a particular system of philosophy or to some particular philosophers, but to philosophy, to reason as such. So both fideism and traditionalism sought the sources of at least all our religious and moral knowledge (there were more extreme claims also) in divine revelation alone and never in any accomplishment of human reason. The official Church was finally as much opposed to these as it was to Hermes and Gunther.[4]

It is entirely obvious both from the context of this plethora of conflicting opinions in the nineteenth century and from the overall direction of the constitution *De fide catholica* itself that Vatican I had to try to outline the delicate relationship between faith and human reason; that it could not and did not settle down quietly to discuss faith itself for its own sake. A later paper deals at length with the subject of Faith and Reason, so we need not delay on this matter. We may simply remark that the description of faith given in Vatican I, in passing, cannot be considered a complete blue-print for a theology of faith. Faith it declared to be a supernatural virtue by which, moved by God and aided by grace, we believe to be true those things he revealed, on the authority of the revealing God.[5] *Of course* the concept of faith in Vatican I is a highly intellectualized one; that appears particularly from the section in which faith and reason are described as two orders of knowledge, distinct not only in principle or source, but in object or content as well.[6] But, given the overall aim of the constitution and the context in which it was issued what else could be expected? More might have been hoped for but less could scarcely have been justified.

Some people might think it unfortunte that wo of the most solemn statements on faith by the Catholic magisterium should seem so intellectualized in conception; that Trent and Vatican I seemed to lean on the side of faith as *belief* in things revealed—notice that neither description speaks of belief in *truths* revealed—the former in combating what it believed to be a reduction of faith, the latter in trying to work out a truly Christian theory of human knowledge. Such people would undoubtedly belong to the number of those who erect their theological structures on the letter of conciliar definitions without critical awareness of the spirit in which these were issued. The spirit and guiding intention of a conciliar declaration can be understood only from the historical context in which it was issued.

Some biblical and traditional theology

Neither from linguistic usage in the sacred books nor from the history of theology could one substantiate the description of faith simply as an intellectual assent to a number of revealed truths on the authority of a God who specifically revealed 'truths' (true statements or propositions); nor could one reduce the will factor to the simple function of moving the intellect to this type of assent. Undoubtedly some lesser theologians, mainly text-book composers in more recent times, did opt for this very restricted concept of faith. Small theologians are like small farmers. Their resources are poor and what they produce will not enable themselves or anyone else to live. The anti-modernist oath issued in a *motu proprio* of Pius X, that compendium of all that was crudest in nineteenth-century theological formulation, did indeed ask us to swear that we would define faith as a true intellectual assent to truth acquired extrinsically, by hearing, by which assent we believe to be true those things said, witnessed and revealed by a personal God, our Creator and Lord, on the authority of the same supremely truthful God.[7] This combined the worst impression of revelation—the words 'dicta, testata, revelata' could scarcely refer to anything other than the spoken propositions—with the most insubstantial concept of faith. But we all duly swore, some of us several times. So much for us. In any case, a brief attempt to achieve a more balanced point of view on faith is evident from the documents of Vatican II. There we read of the obedience of faith which must be given to God, an obedience by which man entrusts his whole self freely to God, offering 'the full submission of intellect and will to God who reveals' and freely assenting to the truth revealed by him.[8] Typical of the compromise nature of Vatican II documents as a whole, this does not achieve a unified and adequate concept of faith but at least—by saying that faith makes a man entrust his whole being to God—it prevents an exclusively intellectualized view of it.

The history of theology does not yield a concept of faith considered exclusively as an intellectual assent to a set of revealed truths. There is time for but one example to illustrate this fact— from Aquinas, who could scarcely be suspected of being anti-intellectual in outlook. Although he does accept a definition of faith as 'cum assensione cogitare'[9] and is prepared to say that what he calls the material object of faith, the material which faith makes its object, includes much more than the 'veritas prima', the first truth which is God himself,[10] nevertheless he insists that all other things are the object of faith only in so far as they have to do with God or belong to our approach to him who is our final goal in life.[11] So it is that Aquinas, in his neat scholastic way, shows up faith as a complexity. On the assurance of the revealing God and driven towards him as our goal in life by the dynamism of our whole nature (here is the will function in faith), we accept all those things revealed about him and about our relationship with him as practical and practicable stages of our journey towards him. Explaining the threefold phrase 'credere Deo, credere Deum, credere in Deum', Aquinas explains succinctly how faith involves reliance on God who is revealed, practical acceptance of what is revealed about himself and us and the consequent dynamism of our driving towards him;[12] three moments inseparable in the one living human actuation that we call faith.

Wherever one goes in the Bible, whether one begins with the Hiphil form of the Hebrew stem which underlies the word 'amen' (the nearest Hebrew equivalent to the word 'faith' and its derivatives), or with the Septuagint or New Testament usage of the word πιστις—one impression is constantly received and as constantly reinforced, namely, that faith is a word like grace. It is a word, that is, which is capable of a most complex range of meanings; a word that would defy any attempt to define it in any single sentence; a word which is capable of development or change in its content in accordance with the changing or developing circumstances in which people use it; a word, in short, the precise meaning of which in any particular instance can only be gleaned from the concrete context in which it is used. Yet there is a logic in the complexity and in the development and anyone who would wish the sacred books to guide his understanding would need to let this logic mould the structure of any concept of faith he might propose. Let us illustrate very briefly from some biblical examples what is meant by this complexity, this development, this logic.

The Hiphil of the Hebrew stem which underlies our word 'amen' means to declare God, *ne'eman*, 'to say Amen to God'.[13] What this means in detail can be gleaned from the context: 'If the reference is to God's requirements, order, or command (*Deut.* 9:23: Ps. 119: 66; 2 k. 14:17), then faith implies acknowledgement of the requirement and man's obedience.'[14] At a time such as that of Isaiah's composition, when the little kingdom of Juda seemed totally at the mercy of neighbouring great powers, faith meant no less than standing firm in the Lord, without fear of men or trust in them. It meant total dependence on God, undoubtedly in recognition of all he had done in the past and of the covenant they said he had formed with them—total dependence for their very continuance (*Is.* 7:9; 7:1 ff.; 30:15). Later still, in the time of Deutero-Isaiah, when Juda too had collapsed, stems that carried the meaning of hope took over the task of expressing man's relationship to God—it was now a matter of 'hope nevertheless'. It is the same relationship but now in recognition of the consequence of man's sin as well as of God's covenant; the same relationship of standing firm still in the Lord, but now in very different historical circumstances. Weiser considers the Hiphil of *'mn* the stem for faith in the Old Testament, because it carried the meaning of man's definitive relationship to God and so directed development of meaning in other stems, such as those for trust and hope. The meanings of these words, by reason of the kind of historical development just briefly outlined, can thus become interchangeable.[15]

In the New Testament πιστεύειν can mean 'to rely on', 'to trust', 'to believe'. It involves now one's relationship to the risen Jesus, acknowledging him as Lord and Saviour, that is, in his own relationship to God his Father. Its reliance and trust content is constant but its recognition content can vary—that is, what is recognized as God's act towards man and man's consequent relationship to God can vary in the conception and expression of different writers. In the fourth gospel, faith approaches very closely to knowledge—for Jesus has allowed us to truly know God and in that our salvation has already begun to exist.[16] In Hebrews, faith can be 'the ground of things hoped for'. For this author Jesus' achievement was to enter the Holy of Holies in heaven and salvation awaits us there with him. Thus faith in this content has a pronounced hope element contained in it. It is recognition that our High Priest and Victim has gone before us into the Holy of Holies and consequent reliance in hope. Finally, one can speak of believing the gospel (1 *Cor.* 15:2), believing *that* Jesus was raised—for most people do not know of Jesus except by listening to those who did. And consequently one can speak of 'the faith', meaning the content of what is preached about Jesus (*Gal.* 1:23), preached so that people would recognize, acknowledge, trust for themselves, hope.

Faith then conveys a complexity of meaning, yet with an inner logic. In a religious context it implies recognition of God or of Jesus on their words or acts or both with consequent dependence of one's life and placing of one's hopes on these. Its precise content varies according to one's historical circumstances and also according to one's conception of what exactly God or Jesus did or said and what exactly this implies for us. For changes occur in men's ideas as well as in their extrinsic circumstances, though the two are closely interlinked.

Finally, by a further logical extension of the meaning of the word, one can speak of 'the faith'; that is, a formulated expression telling all about whom or what one entrusts oneself to, about what was done to elicit such dependence, and the implications of this for oneself and one's destiny.

From all that has been said it is clear that the Bible regards faith as a personal response to God—it is my total reliance on God, acknowledging all that he means to me. Only when I speak of 'the faith' does the word take on a more impersonal aspect, and bring formulated expressions and possibly assent to those more to the fore. But at this stage we are dealing with a logical extension of the core of meaning which the word 'faith' conveys, not with that core itself. It is always necessary to keep that in mind when dealing with faith. Now if the Bible, and the best of later theology, regard faith as personal response through all their historical variations, we must ask the question: what justifies the Bible and the best of later theology in regarding faith as a personal response? We must delve more deeply into the nature of faith.

The concept of faith

In this third, largely analytic part of the paper I want to look just briefly at the elements that go into the make-up of faith. Then I want to ask the question: admitting that the response of faith may differ in content in different historical circumstances, are there yet two radically different kinds of faith: one, the faith of those directly favoured with a divine revelation; the other, the faith of those who listen to the former. After this analysis, in the fourth and final part, it should be possible to say whether and in what sense faith is a personal response.

Let us say, at the risk of oversimplification that there are two elements in faith: recognition, which contains the knowledge element (this can be explicated in terms of what we call truths of the faith) and trust. In religious contexts the recognition has to do with that which is disclosed in man's experience as the ultimate power; and the trust is equally ultimate. I entrust not just some possession or even some loved one but my very existence, my life and destiny. This element of ultimate trusting of self makes the recognition element into an acknowledgement. I don't just perceive some being intellectually or postulate or suppose:[17] I acknowledge, confess, believe some particular being to exist, for always his relationship to me, my relationship of utter existential dependence on him is in view, any conscious reliance on him is merely the acknowledgement of it. The two elements are thus inseparable.

Looked at from the point of view of changing historical circumstances and again at the risk of oversimplification let us say at the outset that there are two different kinds of faith—at least at first sight they look different—before going on to deal with other differences. There is the faith of the man who is actually involved in events in which he considers God himself to be active. Some men were involved in events later recorded as the Sinai epiphany, some were involved in an unexpected escape from Egyptian suppression, some lived through the military, political and administrative success of David and Solomon, some experienced the long insecurity of Juda as a tribute-paying vassal kingdom under the Assyrians, some were uprooted in the Babylonian exile, some came back and tried to rebuild; some shared in the public mission of Jesus, some claimed that he appeared to them after his death.[18]

It is very likely that not all who were involved in those events saw them as acts of God. It is probable that the events themselves could be read by a spectator as unusual but nevertheless natural—with the exception of the last in the list, the resurrection appearances; and these significantly were not historical events in the normal publicly verifiable sense at all (neither of course, was the resurrection itself), though they were historical events in the sense that some actual historical individuals witnessed appearances of Jesus to themselves. It is quite certain that those who did see these events as acts of God and proposed them as such in order to awaken faith in others who either participated but did not see them in this light or did not participate at all, that these privileged ones were much less interested in the precise historical details of these events than they were in the implications of the fact that they saw God active in them—implications both for man's understanding and acknowledgement of God and for the fate of man himself. (This is why it is so difficult for us now to reconstruct an exact historical account of these events, even of the earthly life of Jesus which, of all those mentioned, is closest to us in time.) It is clear, as we have already remarked that the men who did see in these events the activity of God yet formulated their implications in different ways, usually in accordance with the historical circumstances of the time.

So the content of *the faith* changed—by the content I mean the details of what men thought God to be doing, expected him to do, relied on him to do. In the settled kingdom of David they expected God to establish that kingdom forever (2 *Sam.* 7:8 ff.); in the beleagured condition of the vassal statelet of Juda they were asked to trust that Jahweh alone would maintain them (*Is.* 7:9), if only for the purity of the cult (because vassaldom involved admission to the temple of altars to other deities); in the time of the exile they expected God to vindicate them again on some great day of the Lord, and forgive them and even to put a new spirit in them so that misfortune would not recur (Ezekiel). Soon by a gradual refinement of man's moral and religious consciousness, as they gradually focused on the individual man rather than the people as a whole they trusted God to vindicate the individual even beyond death. This hope was given a ground in the appearance of the risen Jesus.

The exilic prophets were the first men of faith to focus on a future day of the Lord. After them some men of faith began to see their experience of present history as one of unremitting suffering and disappointment. These looked to a future intervention of God and their language at least suggested a radical discontinuity with present history. That was their expression of faith and they are known as apocalyptic thinkers. It would be wrong to play down their contribution, if only because, for all the restraint of his own imagery, the historical Jesus was closer to their mentality than to any others of his time; and besides there was a very strong apocalyptic element in New Testament preaching and writing and there is a very strong apocalyptic element in popular and professional Catholic faith to this day. To some 'apocalyptic is the fruit of pessimism',[19] the work of men of faith, yes, but of men who despair of *this* world or *this* history ever coming to any good, even being brought to any good even by God. To some, apocalyptic is simply the attempt to read history from the viewpoint of the decisive end while, in its use of imagery, respecting God's sovereign freedom in regard to the details of that end.[20] It would appear to be almost as much a matter of the man's own temperament as to the difficult nature of the times whether he emphasizes continuity of God's intervention with the present world and present history or seeks to escape into a radically discontinuous world and future, whether he emphasizes salvation here and now (as happens in the fourth gospel), or salvation still to come, while having some place for both.

Finally, differences in conceptions, or pre-conceptions, about the nature of the divinity, the nature of man and the world, also caused differences in the content of faith as formulated and announced by these preachers, prophets and inspired writers. The way in which an early tribesman of Israel will experience and speak about God's salvific action will obviously differ from the way in which a man of hellenistic culture in the first Christian century will experience and speak about God's salvific action. For the primitive tribesman his God is one amongst many, though he may prove himself in conflict the greatest of them all; for Philo God is the one stable reality over against the corruption and flux of this world, so that salvation means resting in him, as opposed to the world. So much for the faith of the man actually involved in events and seeing in these the activity of God himself.

What of those who are not directly involved in events such as those mentioned; what even of those who have been involved but who have been unable or unwilling to see in them the significance and the implications that others saw in them and then proclaimed? What of the faith of such people? Must their faith be, first at least, an intellectual assent to a message *extrinsicum acceptae*, received purely from without, simply *ex auditu*, by hearing the account of the events and their implications preached to them, as these phrases from the Anti-Modernist Oath would certainly suggest? Undoubtedly the men who told and re-told the story of God's mighty acts in Israel and the men who preached the death and resurrection of Jesus expected to arouse faith in their hearers; the men who wrote the accounts of these events and drew out their implications did so with the set purpose of evoking an answering faith in their readers (*John* 20:31), and Paul said explicitly that faith is from hearing (*Rom.* 10:17)—or reading, I suppose too, since he was probably dictating these words to a scribe.

Are there two different kinds of faith then? Is faith a personal response? If so, which kind of faith is a personal response? Both kinds? and to what person or persons? We should not like to allow too dichotomous a distinction between the two different kinds of faith just mentioned; not only because, this would make all attempts to talk about faith difficult, but because it would result in our admitting two very different kinds of religious humanity, with little or nothing in common to unite them. One group would be speaking out of an experience in which the other could have no part; the other would be listening to words that could find no echo in their experience of life. While not wishing therefore to deny that some religious men are more privileged than others—we are not all prophets or inspired writers, we cannot all claim to have had a vision of the risen Lord, and none of us would say that we were in the same class as Jesus of Nazareth—we should like to see some continuity between the two groups. Paul did say that faith was *ex auditu*, but, at a time when distinctions between general and special revelation, or between reason and faith, were not yet in vogue, he could upbraid the Gentiles for worshipping and serving creatures instead of the Creator (*Rom.* 1:25). Even where special events were in question, and not just the works of creation as such, it was clearly the mind of Old Testament writers that those could bring about acknowledgement of God, not simply amongst privileged individuals or amongst those to whom the latter preached, but amongst all kinds of people. So the plagues in Egypt should have caused Pharaoh and the Egyptians to acknowledge God (*Exod.* 7:17; 7:5). In Second Isaiah the activity of Jahweh is to bring about acknowledgement of his deity, not only in the case of Cyrus, who is expected to liberate the captive Jews and restore their place of worship (45:3) but for all peoples (43:10), for all mankind (49:26). There is no thought here of a particular privileged group who would alone be capable of seeing the activity of God in historical events. The possibility is in principle open to all men, though few in fact may realize it.[21]

No man can prove God's existence. If a man could prove God's existence he could then go home, go to bed and forget it, as he could the conclusion of any other piece of theoretical reasoning. But any man may notice the contingency of his own existence, the un-obvious, uncertain, unconfirmed nature of it. He may be driven—invited, inspired (what word can be used here?) to affirm a ground of that existence, which by definition not only holds its present guarantee but its future prospects. He may notice the contingency of his existence and look for its ground and prospects, not in the course of some piece of quiet metaphysical contemplation—though that, too, is possible and even recommended—but in the unquiet of political, military or economic disturbances. In such disturbances he can really feel the contingency of his existence in most concrete form and he can be particularly invited to affirm ground and prospects for it. For this is faith, namely the affirmation, acknowledgement, of a power that sustains our existence in all the concrete circumstances of human living, an acknowledgement that holds out whatever prospects there are for the future of human existence. It is not theoretical knowledge. The most influential religious thinkers in modern times have insisted on this—a whole line of them from Kierkegaard to Tillich—men who addressed *all* their contemporaries and not just an inner circle of their fellow theologians or fellow Church members. The proper response to the question of existence is not a theoretical answer. The *question* is not theoretical. It is *my existence* which is in question. My answer, therefore, cannot take the form of theoretical intellectual knowledge to which I intellectually assent. No, it must be an acknowledgement, an entrusting. As remarked already, a sense of dependence upon, entrusting absolutely to, is inseparable from affirmation of the ground of my being and the hope for my future. All men can have faith, therefore, faith that grows out of their own inner experience of existence in the circumstances of their own times.

Secondly, looked at now from the point of view of particular historical circumstances or events: it is obvious *a priori* that no event which takes place *as part* of the cosmic reality or its history can be more revelatory of God, more self-authenticating as an act of God, more evocative of *the faith* response than cosmic reality itself taken as a whole in all its general, evolutionary and historical dimensions.[22] *A posteriori*, that is to say, from the results of any responsible attempts to reconstruct the actual historical events that underlie the narratives of both Old and New Testament, it is most highly probable that all of them could have been retold by a secular historian, without damage to the substance of these events, but without any necessity, imposed on the researcher by the events themselves, of seeing these particular ones as special acts of God, thus differentiating them absolutely from all others.

There is nothing to differentiate the external history of the kingdoms of Israel and Juda, for instance from the tenth to the sixth century B.C., from the history of any other small people who suffered similar success and failure in history. No more is needed to explain the events than the natural interplay of forces in history. But some men did see God in these events, sustaining them in their existence or punishing them for their infidelities, and that was the faith that distinguished the people as a whole. Nothing prevents its occurrence in other peoples in their own historical circumstances.

Something similar must be said of the earthly history of Jesus of Nazareth. As an externally observable set of events it would not prove that God was in Jesus, reconciling the world to himself. Undoubtedly Jesus made some very strong claims for his own authority in formulating the essentials of a godly life, and the even stronger claim that men's relationship to himself would be decisive for their destinies. But such claims could only be verified in the resurrection and, as already stated, that is not a publicly verifiable event of the usual historical kind. Some men claimed visions of the risen Jesus and thus enabled others to be assured that their faith in *resurrection*, which preceded Jesus and succeeded him, was well-grounded. This was a confirmation of basic, historical faith, not a replacement of it or an extrinsic addition to it. The history and the fate of Jesus is rightly regarded by some men of faith as the unique act of God in human history since it not only shows men the definitive way to live—in loving care for each other as sons of one Father—but shows in anticipation God's definitive victory over man's last enemy, death. A preacher of Jesus as the Christ puts the final touches to the picture of human existence as the man of faith can see it. He is preaching to others a confirmation and definitive form of faith as they can already know it from their own experience. The preacher is confirming and putting final form on what a man can already acknowledge.

Faith a personal response

There are not two entirely different kinds of faith then; one from internal experience of the historical events that condition human existence, the other from external preaching, *ex auditu*. Faith is a possibility for all men that grows out of the historical circumstances of their own life and world. Prophets are always possible. The man who relates to me the facts about the life and destiny of Jesus of Nazareth is attempting to evoke in me faith in a saving God, a faith that is basically possible for me in any case, and he is attempting also to give this faith definitive—that is, Christian, form. If he succeeds in evoking faith in me and particularly if he succeeds in giving my faith Christian form then I naturally join him and his kind. I naturally form common cause, community with him. In a way the faith aroused in me though primarily an acknowledgement of God and of Jesus, is a response to him also, a person-to-person response. But is it a personal response to God?

There has been in recent theological writing—my own included —a tendency to describe man's relationship to God almost exclusively in terms of interpersonal relationships. This has no doubt helped to offset some of the impersonalism of former theology, the vast impersonalism of a juridical system of rights, duties, merits and demerits. It has also allowed celibates to wax ecstatic about the glories of human love, thereby compensating themselves for some of their own lack of it. Too often it over-looked the differences behind the similarities. For God is not a person as humans are and, consequently, we do not know him to be a person and cannot respond to him as to a person in the same way as we can in the case of humans. Perhaps the essential difference lies in that we can treat human persons as objects, at least verify their existence as objects, independently of any personal relationship to them. This is not possible in the case of God. In other words I have no way of establishing the existence of God as an objective fact independently of my own relationship to him—as I can establish the existence of other human beings independently of any relationship of mine to them and then decide whether to approach them on a more personal basis or not. I come upon God only and always as the ground of my life and existence and the ground of my world. I cannot posit God outside of this relationship for this relationship is constitutive of my very being. This, however, does not mean that my relationship to God is the supreme form of intersubjectivity, the purest I-Thou relationship which only the weakness of my nature at times tempts me to objectify—that is, to picture God as if he were an object that could be thought of first in isolation and fully described, and afterwards related to the thinker.[23]

There is no pure, intersubjective relationship between myself and anyone else, God included—as if there were in me, Cartesian style, a purely spiritual ego related directly, without the help of my physical world or the actual events of my life-history, to some other ego. That would make faith, my whole spiritual life— as it is so often mis-named—into a non-worldly, purely subjective type of affair. No, there may be further relationships to God, of which a mystic or a prophet or an inspired man could tell me, but none can be independent of my awareness of God precisely as the source of my life and existence in this physical world and in the context of my own present historical circumstances: there is no relationship to God not first mediated to me through this. Faith then is personal response in this sense: it is a response to an invitation. The invitation comes to me as the sense of the contingency of my existence in all the concreteness of my present historical circumstances. It is an invitation to see my world and my present history grounded in a being I call God and to relate to it as such. Faith is *my response:* my acknowledgement of God as related to me precisely as I am, situated in this present world and my present history, my consequent dependence on God or self-entrusting to God for my present life and my future destiny. My Christian faith is my response to God precisely by responding to my world and my circumstances, my acceptance of this life and history, my acknowledgement of God as ultimate ground of these and final saviour of them, *all* as definitively described for me in the life and teaching, the death and destiny of Jesus. Christian faith is my response to God precisely through my responses to my present world and its concrete historical circumstances as this response is determined for me by the life and fate of Jesus. Hence it is acceptance of Jesus' life and fate—his way—as decisive for my own life and destiny: it is acceptance of Jesus as Lord.

Faith is a response to an invitation that comes to me from God in the very quality of my existence, my historical existence. It is a response to a being whom I can think of analogically as personal. If my faith has Christian form it is a response also to Jesus whom I accept as the Christ. It is a response to Jesus more in his function as revealer and inaugurator of the definitive relationship of man to God, than to the historical 'personality' of Jesus with which I have now no adequate contact. My Christian faith is also my response to those who have carried the message of Jesus' life and destiny to me in order to give my basic faith Christian form. In these ways and with these limitations we may accept the title of this paper: Christian Faith as Personal Response.

Religious Experience and Christian Faith

DONAL J. DORR

THE title of this paper is so general that we shall begin by proposing a subtitle, namely: 'The Objectification of Religious Experience'. This suggests that we are here presupposing that the existence and validity of religious experience have been established: our present concern is to examine the relationship between such religious experience and Christian faith. (We presuppose in fact that religious experience is to be found in two forms: the first is man's search for ultimate foundations, meanings and values—and our conception of this has a lot in common with the account of faith given by Fr Mackey; the second form of religious experience is that of a gracious response on the part of the Transcendent to man's ultimate questions and needs—and our notion of this corresponds in many respects to the account of revelation given by Fr Fransen.) The use of the word 'objectification' in our subtitle indicates that we are thinking here of the Christian faith more as an objective system of doctrine than as a personal religious response; using Fr Mackey's distinction we may say that what is in question is more '*the* Faith' than 'faith'.

The formal treatment of Christian doctrine in terms of its relation to religious experience is relatively recent. Until less than two hundred years ago it was much more closely related to 'rational' philosophy. Christian truths about God were in a certain continuity with the truths of natural theology—even after the Reformers' attacks on reason. But then came Kant, a figure whose importance can scarcely be exaggerated. His *Critique of Pure Reason* was seen as the death-certificate of traditional doctrinal statements. Since the rational-conceptual route to theology seemed blocked, those who wanted to reflect on religion had to look around for some alternative route. Some followed Kant's own lead in deriving religion, and ultimately theology, from morality.[1] But many would hold that in this way religion loses its specific character and is reduced to morality.[2] But an alternative route was found in the analysis of Christian experience Though there were many pitfalls on this new route, the exploration of Christian experience has in fact been of great benefit to theology. Even if one does not agree that Kant's critique blocks the old route, one cannot afford to neglect the new one. For in fact the two routes turn out not to be alternatives running parallel to each other; the starting-point of the old route is the finishing point of the new one. The new route begins at a point much nearer to the modern mentality than the old one so its exploration is a necessary part of the prolegomena to theology in the modern world.

Our paper falls into two parts. The first section is mainly historical; in it we examine the account of religious experience in relation to Christian faith given by Otto, Schleiermacher and Modernism. In the second section we propose an outline for a systematic treatment of religious experience and Christian doctrine.

I: HISTORICAL APPROACH

Otto

The most straightforward way of dealing with religious experience is that adopted by Rudolf Otto in his famous book, *The Idea of the Holy*.[3] Otto's account of the '*mysterium tremendum et fascinans*' is too well known to require elucidation here. But we shall focus our attention on the way in which he overcomes the Kantian barrier. He postulates in man's spiritual equipment, *alongside* the pure and practical reason, a third area which has to do specifically with religion. For Otto, then, there is the religious *a priori* which he insists is not reducible either to knowledge or to morality. The numinous mental state, he says, 'is perfectly *sui generis* and irreducible to any other'.[4] So Otto 'finds the seed of religion in a peculiar *a priori* for the irrational manifestation of the deity'.[5]

Since the central moment of religion is irreducible and unlike
anything else it follows that it cannot be expressed in any set of
concepts. When we speak about the various aspects of the
religious experience, e.g. 'dread',[6] 'stupor',[7] 'entrancement',[8] or
'comfort'[9] we are of course making use of concepts. But Otto
is very insistent that each of these is only 'a sort of illustrative
substitute', an 'ideogram'[10] not a true expression of the particular
emotional moment or aspect of the religious experience. The
concepts are analogies borrowed from 'natural' life; they offer
parallels from the rational side of life for non-rational aspects of
the religious experience.[11] The religious experience cannot occur
on its own; it is combined with, and penetrated by, rational
elements.[12] But no conceptual statement can express it, any more
than the 'natural' feelings expressed in the words of a song can
express the 'non-natural' experience aroused by the music.[13]

Where does this leave us in regard to doctrinal statements?
(i) They may be metaphorical or analogous statements, attempting
to suggest in 'rational' or 'natural' concepts a religious experience
which is 'non-natural' and non-rational, or (ii) they may be true
in the full and proper sense. But then they are, strictly speaking,
non-religious. They merely run parallel to religious experience
touching it at no point. Or (iii) both of these alternatives may
apply. But none of these positions is very attractive. The first
raises major difficulties in regard to the truth of Christian doctrines, and the question of relativism. (This is an issue we shall
discuss later.) The second and third positions both leave us
vainly trying to 'tack together' religion and doctrine. Otto does
not tell us how to relate the 'irrational mysterium' to 'the moral
and rational ideas of God'.[14]

There can be no gainsaying the significance of Otto's analysis
of the experience of the numinous. But his method of circumvent-
ing Kant leaves the philosopher of religion with considerable
difficulties. The very isolation of religious experience as something quite distinct in form and source from any other human
experience gives rise to a particular difficulty in modern times.
For it is precisely this kind of distinct religious experience which
seems to be found irrelevant to modern secular living and which
seems to be disappearing today.

Scheiermacher

In view of the difficulties associated with Otto's position, and the inadequacy of the Kantian framework within which he operates, we are forced to look further than Otto for an adequate treatment of the relation between religious experience and religious expressions or doctrines. An obvious place to look is in the work of Schleiermacher who had a great influence on Otto. In fact Otto believed he was following Schleiermacher in basing religion on a 'new, unique, and independent area of human existence', 'alongside knowledge and action'.[15] But this, as Niebuhr points out, is to misread Schleiermacher.[16] Schleiermacher differs from Otto precisely in not positing a distinct religious *a priori*, and in not placing religion *alongside* gther spiritual activities of man. Where he scores is in locating religion at the deepest level of the conscious subject, prior to any differentiations. Schleiermacher then avoids the difficulties we have noted with Otto's position. This is one reason for studying his work. But, more basically, Schleiermacher cannot be overlooked because to him belongs the credit for the first serious analysis of the subjective and pre-reflective basis for personal religion.[17]

Schleiermacher is popularly known as the theologian of feeling. In the past fifty years or so he has had a 'bad press'. One reason for this is the attack of Barth and his associates.[18] A second reason is that Freudian-type psychology conveys to the popular popular mind a rather jaundiced view of human emotions and seems to present the human psyche as 'a kind of "underground" from which the dogmas . . . of religions arise'.[19] The whole approach to Schleiermacher is far too glib. It cannot be urged too strongly that 'feeling' (Gefuhl) is for Schleiermacher a technical term. He himself was well aware that his position was open to misunderstanding. He endeavoured to avoid this in his later work by using the term 'immediate consciousness' as a synonym for feeling.[20] This brings out the point that for him 'feeling' does not stand for the irrational; rather it is part of rational consciousness.[21] So when Schleiermacher finds the basis of doctrine in religious 'feeling', one is not entitled to accuse him at once of emotivism and consequent subjectivism.

Schleiermacher's 'feeling' has to do with the inner unity of the self.[22] It is, he says,[23] the immediate presence of the entire undivided personal existence, sensible as well as spiritual. It is in Schleiermacher's early work *On Religion*[24] that one gets the clearest account of his position on this matter.[25] He envisages a situation where man is becoming conscious of himself. The movement begins from a moment where there is no distinction between subject and object.[26] The movement is complete once it produces its end product, either in the order of objective knowledge or in the strictly subjective order of feeling.[27] But what Schleiermacher wishes us to focus on is what happens in between: 'You are to apprehend a living movement . . . What you are to notice is the rise of your consciousness . . .'.[28] In this transitional moment the identity of subject and object is preserved but already there is a slight differentiation of the two.[29] It is just at this point that the religious experience is located.

That there are many varieties of religious experience was of course recognized by Schleiermacher. But he believed that they all have one thing in common and that common element is precisely what makes them all be religious in character. What they have in common is the fact that each participates in a primordial religious experience.[30] This primal religious experience is never attained on its own,[31] but its nature can be analysed and this analysis rather than an examination of particular varieties of religious experience, is the way to understand religion.

Already we have seen that what is in question takes place in the human consciousness *on its way* towards explicit self-consciousness. In this moment of blossoming awareness there occurs something that is not quite a feeling and not quite an item of objective knowledge. It is designated 'the feeling of absolute dependence'. This technical term requires explanation. The word 'dependence' is used to denote a being-acted-on by another. The word 'absolute' is used in contradistinction to 'relative' dependence; it indicates that we are dealing here with something of a different order from the 'relative dependence' and 'relative freedom' which is part of everyday living in the world, acting on others (relative freedom) and being acted on by others (relative dependence). What Schleiermacher means is that, over and above our awareness of acting on others and being acted on by them or depending on them, we have accompanying all our activity an awareness that all the activity which springs from ourselves comes ultimately from a source outside ourselves; we are being-acted-on in a primordial way to which no primordial 'freedom' on our part corresponds.[32] Niebuhr calls this the feeling of an 'absolutely original having-been-posited-in-a-particular-way'.[33]

Since this awareness of being ultimately conditioned or dependent occurs in consciousness before one has clearly distinguished subject and object, there is no clear objective knowledge of what it is that causes it or what it relates to. Schleiermacher rejects the approach of idealists like Schelling who posit an immediate intellectual intuition of the Absolute.[34] Nevertheless, the feeling of absolute dependence is a point of contact with God. In fact it is the only valid one. The reason is that every feeling tends *spontaneously* towards expression; and the subject also *deliberately* employs a process of objectification in order to understand his mental states and retain them in the form of thought.[35] This takes place in the case of the 'feeling of absolute dependence'. In order to attain a certain clarity it finds utterance in a 'direct inward expression'; and this is our consciousness of God.[36] So then the idea of God 'is nothing more than the expression of the feeling of absolute dependence'.[37]

It is important to note that there is no possible room for doubt whether God is the correlate of our feeling of absolute dependence; there is no need to *prove* this. This is because the very word 'God' takes its meaning precisely from this feeling and any further comment of the idea of God must be evolved out of this.[38]

When we think or speak of God we have gone beyond the feeling of absolute dependence and are using the idea of God which expresses it. Already at this stage we cannot avoid anthropomorphism and therefore a degree of falsification. For we have moved beyond the state of immediate consciousness where object has not yet been distinguished sharply from subject and where the primal religious 'feeling' is located. We have moved to the realm of clear objective thought (where subject and object are opposed). Here the God-consciousness is, so to speak, contaminated with elements from our everyday objective knowledge of the world.[39] This can be summed up by saying that our true awareness of God is not, strictly speaking, objective (though it is not merely subjective either since it is simply prior to the clear distinction of subject and object); as soon as it is uttered objectively—as it must be—it becomes to some extent falsified. So we must agree with Barth's view that for Schleiermacher the tenets of the faith are only 'derivatives of the original thing, the inner state' and: 'The divine is ineffable'.[40]

The priority given to 'feeling' over formulation is such that for Schleiermacher a particular proposition is dogmatic or theological in the proper sense only when it is derived from religious feeling. A 'speculative' or philosophic proposition derived from 'the purely scientific interest', no matter how similar to, or even indistinguishable from, a truly dogmatic proposition, must always be assumed to be basically different from it, because of its different source.[41]

Schleiermacher gives a sophisticated account of different forms of expression: poetic expression is based on exaltation from within; rhetorical expression is based on interest stimulated from outside, by preaching; finally, descriptive, didactic expression is a derivative and secondary form, emerging in developed cultures as a scientific way of eliminating apparent contradictions in the other two forms of expression.[42] Theology and dogmatics belong to this third form of expression. One can see at once that here we are at two removes from the primal religious revelation. It would be quite wrong to assume that, for Schleiermacher, religious truth is first properly attained at the stage of dogmatic expression, by the elimination of inconsistencies in poetic and historical forms of expression. Quite the contrary. The primal truth is present in immediate consciousness prior to *any* of the forms of expression; and the source of the apparent contradictions is the necessity to objectify and express the primordial truth.

It is just at this point that one must accept or reject Schleiermacher's position. What are the consequences of acceptance? Firstly, one will, I think, be compelled to follow him in seeing dogmatics as expressing in highly articulated form, and systematically organizing, the faith of the Church in the *present* age.[43] 'Schleiermacher . . . insisted simultaneously that theology is only the offspring and servant of popular religion and yet that it must push beyond the level of inherited and popular religious language . . . in order to achieve precision.'[44] Note that the 'push' beyond present popular religion is to attain systematic precision and *not* to bring present religious consciousness into confrontation with a definitive revelation in the past, or with past dogmatic formulations of the revelation. This is quite logical. For if the truth is located primarily in present immediate consciousness and only defectively in any type of conceptual expression, then the truth of present consciousness cannot be judged by any religious expressions from the past. This excludes as more ultimate criteria of truth not only dogmas such as Catholics might invoke but also the appeal to the scriptural revelation which both Catholics and Protestants have traditionally made. So the absoluteness of the scriptural revelation has been replaced (at least in principle) by a historical relativism.

A second implication of accepting Schleiermacher's view on the location of primal truth in immediate consciousness seems to be an even more radical form of relativism. We began our treatment of his position by saying that the accusation of subjectivism is too glibly hurled at him simply because of his use of the term 'feeling'. But now we must conclude that his account of the relationship between religious experience and its expression in conceptual terms does not succeed in avoiding subjectivism. It is quite true that this 'feeling' is not more subjective than objective, since it is prior to the distinction between subject and object.[45] It is also true that this 'feeling' is not irrational in the sense of being a merely 'animal' emotion. But, by locating truth primarily in a personal awareness which is inadequately communicable, Schleiermacher seems to have forfeited the right to use extrinsic criteria (such as doctrinal statements of the community) to judge the orthodoxy of religious expressions of the individual. If the community agree on a doctrinal formula, this can only be because each individual *happens* to find it the closest equivalent to his personal, ultimately ineffable, apprehension of the truth. In effect, the notion of religious truth in any meaningful sense has been abandoned in principle; for it is hard to see how anybody could have, or be shown to have, a false apprehension of revelation.[46] One begins to see the point of Feuerbach's shrewd remark: '. . . where feeling is held to be the organ of the infinite, the subjective essence of religion,—the external data of religion lose their objective value'.[47] This applies as much to Schleiermacher's highly sophisticated 'feeling' as to the crudest form of emotion. Despite its brilliance and valuable insights, Schleiermacher's account of the relation between religious experience and Christian faith must be judged to be basically defective.

Modernism

Catholicism lagged a hundred years behind Protestantism in developing a theology of religious experience. It is true that we find in Möhler a very interesting development of the notion of a Christian sense. In fact he has been accused of 'Schleiermacherism' in his account of faith.[48] But he avoids Schleiermacher's dilemma. For the purpose of Möhler's 'deep interior sense', or 'sure-guiding feeling' is to ensure that the Christian's personal understanding of the written word entirely coincides with the sense of the authors of the Scriptures; and he insists strongly that there can be errors on the part of the individual, in which case the 'general sense decides against particular opinion'.[49]

While speaking about the Catholic contribution to a theology of religious experience we cannot overlook Newman's contribution.[50] It represents a major step towards overcoming a kind of theological rationalism which affected post-Reformation Catholic theology. But Newman did not develop a full theology of religious experience. We have to wait for the Modernist period before this comes to the centre of the stage in Catholic thought.

Modernism was characterized by a confusion in themes[51] which it is almost impossible to disentangle. Furthermore, there were many shades of differences between the various authors associated with the movement. This applies especially to the issue which is our central concern here: the relation between religious experience and doctrinal statements. We do not intend to make an exhaustive study even of this aspect of Modernism. Our aim is rather to indicate the typical Modernist approach and to see what are its implications.

Perhaps we can begin by considering the notion of 'immanent-ism' which the encyclical *Pascendi* considered the positive aspect of Modernism.[52] It would be difficult to find a more confusing word since it conjures up the notion of God or Christ as 'within' the believer.[53] It is necessary to disentangle two strands in the notion of immanentism. The first is the denial of the supernatural which results from explaining religion exclusively in terms of natural religious needs.[54] Recent developments in the theology of grace and the supernatural throw a good deal of light on the half-truth which this position contains.[55]

The second strand in immanentism is directly related to our topic. It holds that religious truth in the proper sense can be located only in the heart of the religious subject. This is because it is basically the non-conceptual grasp of an inexpressible mystery.[56] So the point of contact with the divine cannot be anything so 'extrinsic' as a prophet's message or the dogma of the Church; it has to be *within* each subject.

George Tyrrell gives perhaps the best expression in the Modernist position on this issue. He held that the Christian revelation belongs primarily to the category of personal experience rather than of statement.[57] This helps to explain why Tyrrell could claim that revelation (unlike theology) always remains the same.[58] In finding expression, revelation spontaneously clothes itself in whatever language it finds to hand.[59] Revelation is communicated by 'prophecy'.[60] Theology is an attempt to translate the mysteries of the faith 'from the language of prophecy into that of science and to harmonize these translations within the whole system of our understanding'.[61] This leaves theology at two removes from the primal truth.[62]

For Modernism the primal truth is ineffable, so all conceptual formulations can only be approximations. Their ultimate purpose cannot be to contain revelation. But they are required (i) to protect the religious experience in which revelation is accomplished by giving it a conceptual shield, (ii) to recall the religious experience of the apostles, and (iii) to give us the opportunity to evoke an analogous experience.[63]

Since the believer's contact with God does not have a representational character,[64] revelation has to come primarily through the medium of 'feeling'. We shall concentrate on the views of Tyrrell who has the clearest and most developed account of feeling. He speaks of 'a feeling, not a blind feeling, but . . . a felt truth, a felt reality; . . . a feeling which implies and demands a truth'.[65] To understand what he means by this we must have recourse to the psychology he elaborated—a psychology quite different from that of Schleiermacher. Briefly, Tyrrell identifies feeling as a *spiritual faculty* alongside intellect and will. To this extent his view is not unlike that of Otto. But he insists at the same time that the distinction between intellect, will and feeling is a mere work of abstraction, for convenience of speech and reflex thought.[66] 'Thought, Feeling, and Will, the components of the spirit-life, are correlative and inseparable . . .'.[67] Religion involves all three in a living unity; and any attempt to reduce it to one of them is doomed to failure,[68] for '. . . it is only the unbroken unity of the living whole which appeals to the heart and Faith is of the heart'.[69]

Tyrrell cannot then be accused of a crude sensism when he gives such prominence to feeling in religious living. For he is thinking of feeling as a spiritual faculty, inseparable in reality from intellect and will. His notion of a 'felt truth' can be related to his view that the '*vérité pensée*' or explicit understanding is distinct from, and comes later than, the '*vérité vécue*' or lived truth which is holiness.[70] So Tyrrell can say that 'the feeling is full of implicit judgements and practical consequences that are first brought to light by their conflict with the judgements of reason.[71] That feeling takes precedence in such conflicts is evident from Tyrrell's claim: 'What I *feel* about life may be truer than what I say or think about it—even to myself, i.e. it may be the product of a truer, though of an obscure and inexpressible intuition.'[72] This is an echo of Pascal's profound statement: 'The heart has its reasons which the reason does not know.' It is flashes of insight of this type which make Tyrrell so significant; if his psychology is judged to be unsatisfactory at least the alternative ought to ring as true as his to the realities of life.

In the light of Tyrrell's psychology of feeling we can see the inadequacy of a facile criticism of modernism as mere theological pragmatism. Tyrrell himself expressly repudiates the type of pragmatism which makes the truth of a dogma simply and only practical, an ethical myth. He adds: 'I have insisted that a belief which constantly and universally fosters spiritual life must be so far true to the realities of the spiritual world, and must therefore possess a representative as well as a practical value.'[73] This is important because it suggests that it is not quite enough to say, as we said earlier, that conceptual formulations protect, recall and evoke religious experience. They do in fact express certain truths about spiritual realities.

However, this expression of truth is only analogous or symbolic. Tyrrell makes this quite clear in a classic statement of the Modernist position which comes immediately after the remarks just quoted:

> Still I have equally insisted that such representations are almost necessarily analogues or even symbols. And since there may be two analogies of the same truth, whose literal values are contradictory, it follows that 'The Law of Prayer' might easily give us very different creeds of just the same religious value— all equally true to the practical needs of the spirit-life, and analogously representative of the spiritual world.[74]

This is a clear statement of a relativist position in regard to dogmatic formulas. This in turn implies 'an agnosticism which embraced everything but the religious sense itself'.[75] Indeed *Pascendi* saw at the very basis of Modernist, 'a theory of agnosticism and the inability of reason to go beyond the phenomena',[76] and its condemnation was largely on this basis.[77]

It is not surprising that Church authorities reacted so strongly to Modernism. They realized that the very basis of Catholicism, its dogmatic character, was under attack. But the theology of the period was in no position to offer a satisfactory alternative. Instead, harsh disciplinary measures were used to kill Modernism. Forty years ago Riviere had no doubt that it was dead.[78] But anybody aware of current trends must know by now that the skeleton has remained in the cupboard and the ghost has returned to haunt the Church. It has been said that Modernism proposed wrong solutions to problems which it had grasped aright.[79] The biblical problems raised by the Modernist scholars were eventually dealt with on the intellectual level after edicts from the Biblical Commission had failed to solve them. So too the psychological, philosophical and theological issues raised by Modernism cannot be met by disciplinary rules but only at their proper intellectual level. This work has only just begun.

II: SYSTEMATIC APPROACH

Our criticism of Schleiermacher and Modernism is not to be taken as implying that we disagree with their fundamental aim of showing that dogmatic or theological formulations, statements of the Christian faith, are in some sense objectifications of personal religious experience. Catholicism has for so long stressed the objective aspect of the Christian religion that the attempt to find the subjective pole of dogmatic statements seems to smack of immanentism or Modernism. But this is a mistake. The fact is that without reference to religious experience one can have metaphysics but not theology in the full sense; for theology is reflection on religion.[80] So our purpose in the following pages is in many ways similar to that of Schleiermacher and the Modernists, though our conclusions are not the same. We shall examine the process by which the personal experience of having the love of God poured into one's heart (*Rom.* 5:5) gives rise to conceptual statements of doctrine or theology.

Christianity and the other religions

At once this raises a very important question of approach. Is it licit to ask first about religious experience generically and then consider Christianity as a specific instance of the general class of religions? Karl Barth and his associates would of course reject such a procedure out of hand.[81] For them Christianity is the very antithesis of 'religion'. They see religion as a purely human attempt to reach the divine—an attempt doomed to failure and resulting in the erection of an idol. We cannot accept Barth's view, and in a few moments we hope to show why. But first it must be noted that to take the Christian religion as one instance of the class of religions can also give wrong impressions.

It can easily lead one to overlook the decisive difference between Christianity and other religions—a difference which we hope to clarify in terms of two types of revelation.

In recent years it is becoming increasingly evident that Barth's rejection of Christianity as a religion, while it contains a germ of truth, was a blind alley for theology. The Barthian approach tends to leave no point of entry for Christian faith into day-to-day human living. Barth, of course, maintains that God intervenes to provide the entry-point. But even assuming that this can be done it still seems to leave faith and secular life largely irrelevant to each other.[82]

Furthermore, Christians are beginning to take more seriously the fact that we live in a very pluralist world. This fact has to be brought into relation at the theological level with the doctrine of God's universal salvific will and the basic Catholic position that we do not have a two-tier salvation (natural and supernatural) or a two-tier world. Natural religion is a possibility but we can know little about it 'for in the existing world-order true religion is supernatural'.[83] What emerges from this conjunction is a very determined attempt to work out a theology of implicit faith or 'anonymous Christianity'; and Barth's exclusivist position seems less attractive than ever. Fortunately, recent advances in the study of world religions offer the opportunity of taking the notion of implicit faith out of the realm of abstract theory and into the concrete world. Here one finds a multitude of religious systems, each with its own tradition, its history, its developments and its aberrations. The problem is to find in this welter of conflicting religions certain common elements which articulate, verbally or vitally, a truly salvific supernatural faith.

A notable step in this direction has been taken by Friedrich Heiler.[84] He has isolated seven 'principal areas of unity which the high religions of the earth manifest'.[85] Briefly, these are (i) the transcendence, and (ii) the immanence of the divine, (iii) its goodness, truth and beauty, and (iv) its reality as ultimate love; the fact that the way of man to God is (v) one of sacrifice and (vi) always at the same time the way to the neighbour, and that (vii) the most superior way to God is love. Bernard Lonergan suggests that these seven elements are implicit in the religious experience of being in love with God; and he goes on to propose that one would expect the same common element to be found even in the more elementary religions.[86] In this way he finds the basis for what he calls 'universalist afaith'.

Perhaps this whole approach appears naively optimistic and too facile in picking out common elements in the religions while ignoring their very basic differences. But it is not necessarily so. If religions are taken as so many static essences one may find truly essential differences in them. But if they are taken as developing, historical realities, one can attain a much richer understanding, one which goes to the roots. Then one can see the development of characteristic features and realize that there may be a common basis for features which appear now to be essentially opposed. Furthermore, one can handle the issue of aberrations in religion, so that one can distinguish true developments from mis-developments and thus avoid mistaking an aberration for an essential element. In this way one can prescind from false developments and set out to discern the fundamental directions in which the various religions are tending.

The crucial question arises at this stage. How is one to explain the fact that the religions have these major areas in common, or at least have an in-built tendency to move towards these positions? Here one must tread cautiously to avoid the two extremes of rationalism and traditionalism. Many suggestions have been put forward which avoid these extremes: some authors explain common elements in terms of natural religion while others rely on the memory of a primeval revelation made to the first men; but these are not very satisfactory positions. The most promising approach to the question is that which analyses the nature of religious love.

Religious love

The love of God is poured into the heart of the religious man by the Spirit who is given to him (*Rom.* 5:5). We must take seriously the implications of this statement. First of all, there is every reason to believe that this occurs even outside the visible boundaries of Christianity. This means that non-Christians too can receive this supernatural grace; there is no question of explaining their religion in purely natural terms.

A second point to note is that this religious love does not come along merely through personal efforts; it comes as a gift into man's heart. By the 'heart' is meant, of course, the core of the personality of the existential subject. The point of the word 'existential' here is to bring out the fact that we are speaking not of the subject as merely experiencing or understanding or judging, but as actually committing himself, transcending himself in a way that is real and not merely cognitive. And religious love, unlike merely human interpersonal love, involves a self-transcendence which is unrestricted in scope and direction.

There follows a third important point. Religious love is in some sense a source of knowledge. Normally love is the fruit, rather than the source, of knowledge: 'nihil amatum nisi praecognitum'. But in this case the dictum is 'outflanked'.[87] The old-fashioned 'faculty psychology' cannot explain how this takes place. But recently a lot of valuable work has been done on the question of the apprehension of values. A true phenomenology of the existential subject reveals that there is a *spontaneous* attraction towards values of all kinds, and a corresponding aversion from disvalues. As spontaneous, it is a matter of feelings. Our feelings can then be intentional responses to values.[88] If they have been properly 'educated' they incline us to appreciate a true work of art, to respond correctly in delicate inter-personal relationships, to 'sense' what is the morally good course of action in concrete situations, and so on. What we are speaking of here is that 'connatural knowledge' of which the ancients spoke and which was so difficult to account for in terms of the older psychology.

When the existential subject is in love his whole conscious life, spontaneous and deliberate, is gathered up into a unity. His feelings as well as his will are focused on the one he loves. As intentional responses, his feelings give him practical guidance in how to live out his love. In this sense they are a real source of knowledge. His love, however, is the more ultimate source of this practical knowledge, since it is his love which gives rise to his spontaneous feelings.

Religious love, like purely human love, unifies the whole

personality and directs it outwards. It affects the spontaneous life of the conscious subject as well as his deliberate thoughts and actions. Feelings and desires flow from it. These are intentional responses of the religious subject; they incline him towards appropriate ways of manifesting his love of God. In this way there is a spontaneous discernment of values and disvalues flowing from religious love. Needless to say, there is no question here of compulsion: the subject may refuse to allow the direction indicated. Nor is there any question of infallibility: the spontaneous feelings may lead one astray, or, more frequently, incline one towards a certain exaggeration. And these feelings must be nurtured carefully if they are to develop into the sensitive antennae we need in daily living. It is only too easy to muffle them or attune them wrongly. If one thinks, as one must, of the divine action taking effect through these feelings as well as in more deliberate conscious acts, then one can speak of 'grieving the Spirit' by failing to co-operate with and develop this delicate value-sensing equipment we possess. If on the other hand one allows free rein to the Spirit-given love in one's heart then one can make enormous advances in value-sensitivity; we can all think of saintly people who display remarkable knowledge and wisdom which never came to them via their reason. Such people can truly be said to be led by the Spirit, for the source of their knowledge is his outpouring of love into their hearts. (This does not, of course, preclude particular transient inspirations of the Spirit.)

We can now recall Tyrrell's 'felt truth' which we described earlier. One can agree with his statement without accepting his psychology or the basic conclusion which he draws. There is indeed a *vérité vécue* prior to *vérité pensée*; it is indeed true that what I feel about life may be truer than what I say or think about it. In this Tyrrell was right as Pascal was when he said: 'The heart has its reasons which the reason does not know.' But one does not have to hold, as Tyrrell did, that feeling is a spiritual faculty. More important still, one does not have to conclude that religious truth is ultimately ineffable, that it is attained only in an obscure and inexpressible intuition.

This conclusion is implicit in what we have said already.

However, we must now develop and apply it.

Religion as a way of life

We have found that religious love is a source of knowledge. This is a practical knowledge of values and disvalues, good and evil.[89] It accounts for the common areas in the various religions— areas which, significantly, have to do with orientations of the subject rather than the more theoretical aspects of doctrine. This brings home to us that the first and most obvious objectification of religious experience is not a doctrine but a way of life. This statement is of considerable importance for us. It enables us to avoid many of Schleiermacher's difficulties, especially the relativism which we found to be implicit in his position. For a way of life is a public, social, and even historical reality; doctrines are the result of reflection on these social realities, not simply objectifications of private religious experience. However, as yet we are a long way from conceptual doctrines; we are still speaking of a religious way of life.

The love which the Spirit pours into the heart of the religious man is all-embracing in its scope. It is not a narrowly 'religious' thing, unrelated to everyday living. On the contrary it 'invades' the existential subject in the core of his personality where all aspects of his life are centred. So it is possible, at least in principle, for an individual or a community to live the life which flows from religious love without ever envisaging a distinction between the religious and the secular. In this case religious experience is objectified solely in everyday living. However, it is doubtful if any human community ever lived long in this undifferentiated state. (In passing, it might be suggested, very tentatively, that perhaps particular individuals in the modern secularized world are living in this situation; institutional religion may mean absolutely nothing to them so it is not associated with their personal religious experience; but one notes that there is a tendency for even secularized people to differentiate in the way we shall mention.)

The work of men like Mircea Eliade illuminates for us the tendency found in all human communities to differentiate between 'the sacred' and 'the profane'.[90] The sacred will be all that is associated with ultimate realities and values; the profane will have to do with more immediate, everyday things. But the latter will always be seen to derive their meaning, and have their foundation and exemplar in the sacred.[91] The purpose of the distinction is to enable people to understand themselves, to grasp the meaning of their way of life, to reveal the realities they consider fundamental, the values which are their ultimate concern. Even in the more 'primitive' cultures the distinction between what is ultimate or primary and what is derivative or secondary is made; and it operates very effectively; it becomes part of the experienced world. But here the distinction is not worked out in conceptual terms. These meanings, like all others, are felt and intuited and acted out; they are not reflected on, isolated for inspection, or scientifically organized, since the 'undifferentiated consciousness' of the community never envisages such operations.[92]

In 'primitive' cultures, religion is totally dependent on symbols. It is only through the symbol that the Transcendent, the Other, can become present to such people. These people do not isolate meaning and truth from the concrete imaginative presentations in which they are discerned by the human mind. But the Transcendent is not embodied. How then can it be grasped by these people? Through a hierophany. The transcendent meaning or truth becomes associated with some object, place or time in our world, which thus becomes a symbol of the Transcendent.[93] So the symbolic object conveys the transcendent meaning, truth or value to the undifferentiated consciousness.

Symbolic meaning is not something added on to literal meaning as a kind of 'optional extra'. Rather, literal (especially scientific) meaning is a later development, a product of the differentiated consciousness which can disentangle different levels of meaning and focus on one of them.[94] For 'primitive' people the sacred is an omnipresent horizon[95] to all their meaning and acting. All their meanings are multivalent. *Anything* can then be made a specific symbol of the transcendent order by, so to speak, concentrating on its religious overtones of meaning and giving these more importance than the more everyday meaning of the object. Different cultures will 'adopt' different symbols, elaborate different rites and recount different myths. But this does not necessarily mean that some are true and others false. There is room for a pluralism of systems; for the same transcendent meaning, truth or value may be conveyed by a variety of different symbols.

This has important and interesting implications. We have been accustomed to speak of 'pagan' religions as *false*. The question arises whether this is an appropriate word. We can, of course, use it if we mean that these religions do not possess the revealed truth of Christianity; but then 'incomplete' would be more apt a word than 'false'. We can also apply the word 'false' to indicate that they suffer from certain aberrations; but it is not the best word for this—it is too absolute. Most commonly what the word implies is that these people worship *false* gods. This is incorrect (apart from aberrations, which in any case would rarely if ever involve total distortion). The mistake stems from a confusion of symbolic meaning with literal meaning; more basically it comes from imposing our differentiated categories of literal meaning and truth on a situation where they are not applicable. The result is that the symbol is taken for an idol, a false god; and the religion is condemned as a false religion. We hope to suggest that the missionary motivation of Christians is not founded on such insulting oversimplifications.

Shift to theory

We have spoken of the objectification of religious experience in concrete living and of the symbolic knowledge which arises out of the differentiation between sacred and secular. Now we move on to consider how doctrinal knowledge results from a further differentiation. A decisive moment in the development of a culture occurs when people begin to ask questions of the type asked by Socrates and Plato: 'what is justice?' 'what is the state?' and so on. For such questions are not answered merely by giving concrete instances. The questioner has reached a state of differentiation of consciousness where he can distinguish the idea as such. He wants to understand the essential nature of things; he wishes to isolate for closer analysis that which is realized concretely in each instance. This is a step back from the concrete, the immediate, the practical. But it is enormously significant even from a practical point of view. If men had never asked about the atomic structure of the world, atomic energy would never have been harnessed; if 'theoretical' questions about the laws of economics had never been asked, it would not be possible to work out policies to control inflation; the applications of theory to practice are endless.

This shift towards theory (*die Wendung zur Idee*)[96] occurs not only in regard to physical, biological and economic realities but also in regard to the basic foundations and ultimate values of the culture itself. It is then a moment of withdrawal from day-to-day living in which people seek to grasp reflectively the meaning of their lives, their origins, their ultimate concerns and the means employed to attain them. It is a movement from lived experience towards explicit knowledge. As such it is the first step in the emergence of doctrine and theology from religion.

How does this movement from experienced religious living to explicit religious knowledge take place? In much the same way as the development of knowledge takes place in other areas: by the examination of many instances, by learning what is relevant to many, by eliminating what is found to be merely accidental. As a religious tradition is handed on from one generation to the next, reflection on it can result in the building up of a body of knowledge which can also be transmitted to the next generation. If the religion succeeds in crossing over from one culture to another, the explicit knowledge of it can make remarkable advances, for the merely accidental features are less likely to be reproduced in the other culture. Inversely, it is almost impossible for a religion which does not have some body of explicit knowledge of itself to cross such a cultural boundary without suffering 'a sea change into something new and strange'; it will lose its essential meaning[97] or, more likely, become merely one element in a syncretistic religion.

The movement from experience of religion to understanding of religion took a classicist form in the past; but now, like every other human science, it is affected by the modern ideal of science which is empirical rather than deductivist, seeks to handle the contingent rather than looking for necessity, is content with verified probability rather than absolute truth.[98] This change is seen as a threat by some, but in reality it is a challenge which is rich in possibilities. However, this is not the place to pursue this question.

In the movement towards truthful expression of religion there are several possible degrees of differentiation. (i) A first stage is a 'prophetic' type of statement where the meaning and truth are conveyed descriptively and by means of metaphors and symbols. (ii) A more differentiated stage occurs when the attempt is made to express the meaning and truth accurately and unambiguously by the use of technical 'scientific' terms and explanatory concepts. Most of the developed religions of the world have, at least at times, moved towards such usage. (In Christianity the first completely clear instance of it was the introduction of the word 'homoousios' at the Council of Nicea; the controversy about the use of the *word*, as distinct from the doctrine, indicates the novelty of the approach.) (iii) A third stage in differentiation is the making of a clear distinction between theology and dogma. Both of these are located within the world of 'theory', where accurate, non-metaphorical, expressions are being used. The difference between them stems, not from the type of meaning which is involved but from the status of the statements in relation to truth. Dogmas will be affirmations which are judged definitively to be true. Theology will be a search for understanding; as such it will, like other sciences, propose hypotheses which are possible meanings, and then attempt to verify the hypothesis. In this way theology can give rise to statements of dogma. But it is important to note that the verification of a hypothesis which results in its being accepted as a true doctrine is bound up with concrete religious living.

Doctrine as normative

The most important thing to note about doctrinal statements is that they are normative. In its reflection on religious living the community slowly and painfully learns to discern what is essential and what is merely accidental, what is good (in the sense of expressing and promoting religious living) and what is evil from a religious point of view. This knowledge can be expressed in formal statements which are true and which can provide direction and guidance to individuals, and to succeeding generations. They will provide the basis for an 'education' of religious sensitivities or feelings of people. In this sense they take priority over purely individual responses. It is true that personal religious experience gives one a sense of entering a new world, grasping new truths. But no special infallibility attaches to such sensations: one cannot assume that this new vision will, spontaneously or through deliberate reflection, crystallize into a set of true propositions.

On this issue there is a sharp disagreement between our account and that of Schleiermacher and the Modernists. The question hinges on the nature of truth and the role played by theology in the search for, or expression of, truth. For Schleiermacher and the Modernists, theology is at two removes from the primal truth; it is an attempt to systematize and clarify prophetic-type expressions of an experienced truth which in fact is basically ineffable, not adequately conceptualizable—even in prophetic form. For us, theology indeed has its basis in religious experience; but the primal truth is not located there. Theology is indeed an inadequate expression of the truth; but that is because it has not reached its goal of a complete set of dogmas; and because our natural knowledge is inadequate and our supernatural knowledge in this life is of faith ('universalist' or Christian) rather than of 'vision' or infused understanding. Theology must frequently be satisfied to attain an understanding which is analogical. But we cannot agree with those who see little or no difference between analogy and mere metaphor or symbolism.[99] The central point is that a doctrinal statement expressing an analogical under-standing can be *true*—and not a mere 'symbolical expression' of the truth. No single statement of ours ever claims to express all of the truth; but we can make particular true judgements about atoms or anatomy; and we can also make particular true judge-ments about te transcendent world.

For Schleiermacher and Modernism truth is found primordially in the religious experience, prior to all explicit questions and answers. For us, truth as a human possession is located formally in judgements. Reality, any reality, is consciously attained not in experience but in a true judgement.[100] For any Christian, but especially for a Catholic, this disagreement is fundamental. Our position offers an opening for a historical revelation on which is normative in character. The other positions, as has emerged from our study, do not. Having discovered the revelation of the love of God in the heart of man as a source of religious knowledge, they fail to leave adequate room for the further normative revelation which finds its centre in Christ, is expressed in sacred Scripture, is proclaimed officially by the teaching Church, and is accepted in faith by Christian believers.

Need for Christian revelation

Our account of the move from religious experience and concrete religious living to doctrinal statements has been such as to apply to the religion of any culture which has made considerable advances in differentiation of consciousness. It is time to approach the question of the distinctive element in Christianity. We do this by noting some characteristic features of any religious doctrine which does *not* make the kind of claim made by Christianity.

Is it possible for a religion such as we have described so far to make definitive doctrinal statements? This requires a very naunced answer. Natural knowledge of God is a possibility; Catholics are committed to this proposition.[101] So in principle it is possible that different religions could come to make definitively true statements about God on the basis of this knowledge derived from the world. Grace would be required, of course, but the content of the knowledge would be natural. However, as we noted already, there is in the present world no such thing as natural religion. So what we have been dealing with is a set of doctrinal objectifications of *supernatural* religion, divinely-infused love. Our question is whether it is possible to say definitively that certain of these are true and others false, without invoking any further type of revelation.

A first answer is that it is possible to exclude certain formulations as false. For instance, it is possible, at least in principle, to discover that it is false to say that God is in no way immanent in our world; or again it is false to say that God is in no way transcendent; or to deny the necessity for self-sacrifice in coming near to God. The 'discovery' would be made on the basis gf an examination of actual religions, an examination which would indicate the compatibility or incompatibility of such a normative statement with concrete religious living. One would find, of course, that certain religions have tended to adopt such false doctrines; but a dialectical analysis would explain how this happened, and indicate that these religions survived and flourished in spite of, rather than because of, these false doctrines.

If a certain doctrine is false then its converse is true. But the matter is not quite as simple as it seems. The exclusion of doctrines which can be shown to be false (through incompatibility with living religion) may leave one with true propositions which are not very satisfactory. A statement which is true may be so meagre in content, so confused in meaning, so poorly formulated, that it can be misleading in practice and unsatisfactory in the theoretical world. It will be open to constant, and very radical, correction and development. This process may be so upsetting that it is a real hindrance to religious living. The gulf between theory and practice, between theologians and religious people, becomes almost unbridgeable; and the results in both camps are disastrous. So, even at its very best, the process of objectifying religious experience runs into serious difficulties. These are multiplied by the havoc wrought by evil in the religion itself as a way of life and in the hearts and minds of the theologians who are reflecting on it.

Furthermore, a certain plurality of doctrinal systems is concretely inevitable. Doctrinal statements are rooted in living religion. There is a plurality of concrete religions, based ultimately, as we noted earlier, on the arbitrary character of any symbol of the divine. So one expects a diversity of doctrinal systems which even the universalizing drive of theology does not eliminate. A pluralism of cultural systems is undoubtedly a good thing. But a conflict about the nature of ultimate values does not make for harmony. As mankind moves from the isolation of autonomous socio-cultural groupings towards the era of 'planetary man' the situation becomes highly unsatisfactory. For each doctrinal system will have its own set of moral implications and in certain areas of conduct the consequences of one's actions are global—especially in view of modern power over nature and modern techniques of communication. It is not easy to see on what rational basis one might decide that one system is 'true' and the others 'false'—or at least not without long, bitter experience over a period of time which mankind cannot spare.

It seems reasonable, then, to conclude that there is real need for some further supernatural intervention by God in man's affairs. That this has occurred is the contention of Christianity. The second intervention brings the first to its proper fruition; in the light of the second the first can be seen to have been preparatory both in the history of the world and in the hearts of many individuals who come in adulthood to the full Christian faith.

God's first word to us is the universe he has created; when he pours out his divine love into our hearts it is not to take us out of the world but to enable us to live authentically in it. But the extent of the world and the enormous length of history make it almost impossible for us to read aright the message of God's cosmic word, the universe.[102] The explicit revelation will provide men with certain strategic judgements which they can affirm to be certainly true—judgements which can function as foundational for authentic human living on a global scale. In this way is overcome the problems we have noted—problems posed by doctrines which must be open to radical revision, by the invasion of evil into religion and theology, and by the clash of opposing religious and moral systems in a world grown too small to contain them all.

God's first religious intervention is associated with the Holy Spirit: it is he who pours the divine love into our hearts (*Rom.* 5:5). This is to be expected, for he is divine love personified. The second intervention has to do more explicitly with meaning and truth rather than love. One is not surprised then to find that the central role is played in this case by the word of God. In him the universe was created; now he comes to reveal the central aspects of its meaning.

Christ came to enlighten mankind. But in doing so he operated a divine 'economy'—taking this word in its everyday sense as well as as its theological sense. The plan involved an arrangement which respected the order of the world and intervened in each case only as much as was appropriate. So Christ came on earth only once and stayed here in visible form for only a limited time.

The meaning and truth he revealed are passed on first by privileged witnesses and then by a teaching Church.

What are the appropriate interventions in this divine economy? There must first be a prophetic light granted to the privileged witnesses to know with certainty the correctness of the message they proclaim to be the word of the Lord. There must, secondly, be a divine guidance to enable the historical Church to preserve and develop the message that is to be handed on to all generations. This help, like the prophetic light, will have to do with making true statements, so we find here the basis for infallibility of the Church in its dogmatic declarations. Since the Church aims to be transcultural in character the statements in question are more scientifically theological in character than those of the prophets or first witnesses. Thirdly, there will have to be a special divine intervention in the minds of those who hear the message. Again it has to do with reaching the truth. When formally expressed, truth is located in the judgement. So the formal analysis of faith posits the light of faith as divine assistance in grasping as true the message that is heard. In concrete Christian living, however, the truth of the faith is felt and intuited and lived out by the existential subject. So the light of faith permeates the whole personality.

We spoke earlier of the role of the religious symbol in conveying religious truth to people of undifferentiated consciousness. We then moved on to examine the question of religious truth in differentiated consciousness. Lest it be thought that this implies that religious symbols are no longer required once a culture has made this advance, we should like to stress here, that religious symbols are of enormous importance for every religious person, for every Christian. From all we have said it will be evident that we cannot accept in principle the view of Eliade [103] and Ricoeur[104] that the full *meaning* of the symbol cannot be attained non-symbolically. We would hold, however, that the *effect* of the symbol can be attained in no other way. For the symbol conveys many levels of meaning in a unified and concrete way to the whole man; it ensures that no gulf develops between what man knows and what he feels; and in this way it promotes a unification of the personality which is necessary if religion is to be effective in one's life. It is for this reason that the finding of religious symbols for modern man is one of the most pressing tasks of Christianity today.

We conclude by recalling the main points which have been discussed:

We maintained that an important part of the prolegomena to dogmatic theology, especially in modern times, is an examination of the relation between doctrinal statements and religious experience.

We examined the approach of Otto, Schleiermacher and Modernism to this question; we found them very helpful in many ways but incorrect on certain crucial points.

We went on to maintain that Christianity has much in common with other religions; and we found the basis for a 'universalist faith' in the love of God which is poured into the heart of the religious man by the Spirit.

We attempted to show how this love is the source of a practical knowledge through the spontaneous apprehension of values and disvalues.

We moved on to note that the primary objectification of religious experience is religious living; we considered the differentiation between the sacred and the secular; and we spoke of the symbolic knowledge of the transcendent which is all that 'primitive' religions can provide.

We spoke of the shift to theory characteristic of differentiated consciousness and examined how it leads to the elaboration of formal doctrine and the whole theological enterprise.

We stressed the normative character of doctrinal expressions and took issue on this point with Schleiermacher and Modernism; we found that the issue hinged on the nature and 'location' of truth.

Our view of truth as situated formally in true judgement rather than experience left the way open for the historical Christian revelation of truth; we discussed the need for such a revelation. We pointed out briefly the main characteristics of such an 'economy' of interpretative revelation.

Finally, we noted that religious symbols retain their importance so that it is a matter of urgency to develop symbols appropriate to modern man.

The Act of Faith in the Reformed Tradition

HENDRIKUS BERKHOF

Personalization

One of the main elements which caused the rupture in the Western Church was a radically new concept of faith. It is well known that Luther attributed a decisive role to the words of Romans 1:17: 'The righteous through faith shall live.' Following St Paul, Luther understood this quotation from the prophet Habakkuk as meaning: through the act of faith, of faithful surrender to the grace of God, man receives justification, the right relation to God as the guarantee of eternal life. This conviction of Luther is common and basic in the whole Reformation. We might quote here an endless series of devotional, theological and confessional statement. We choose as a typical example the definition of Calvin, who among the Reformers is outstanding for clear and profound formulation. He builds the famous chapter De Fide in his *Institutio* around the following definition:

> We shall have a correct definition of faith if we say that it is the firm and certain knowledge of God's goodness to us which is founded on the truth of his gratuitous promise in Christ, and which is revealed to our minds and sealed on our hearts through the Holy Spirit.[1]

Insights and utterances like this had a revolutionary effect on the first decades of the sixteenth century. They meant a radical break with an age-long tradition. In medieval theology and devotion after the *Sententiae* of Petrus Lombardus the concept of faith did not play that central role; it was understood as an initial stage in the process of grace; an act of man's intellect by which he submits himself to the authority of the Church and accepts her doctrine. As an act of the intellect faith must be complemented and elevated by an act of the will, i.e. the supernatural virtue of faith must be surpassed by the supernatural virtue of love. Without that, faith is incomplete; faith-without-form (*fides informis*), it is not yet formed i.e. animated, or made living, by charity (*fides caritate formata*). Faith-without-form is a mere outward act, an assent (*assensus*), a historical faith (*fides historica*), which in its minimum form, is even acceptable as implicit faith (*fides implicita*) as a faith which hardly knows its object, the revealed truths, but believes that what the Church knows about it must be the truth.

Why did the Reformers reject this concept so vigorously? As far as I can see, they did so for the following three reasons which are interrelated:

First, this kind of faith is impersonal; man is not involved as a whole, and by implicit faith can even hide himself in the collectivity of the Church. Secondly, this kind of intellectual assent is man's own work over against God's work. It is a work by which man initiates a process of grace in which through his faith and love, he plays a co-operative and even meritorious role. Thirdly, as soon as man discovers that through his radical estrangement from God he is unable to understand the truth of God and to co-operate with his will, the traditional shallow and meritorious concept of faith will throw him into despair.

According to the new concept, faith is that act by which the sinner unconditionally and radically surrenders himself to the promises of God in Christ, the promises of forgiveness of sins, of justification of the godless, of adoption as children of God, and of the inheritance of eternal life. Faith is a radical and personal act of the whole man, by which he responds to God's grace and enters into the right relation with him. The main contribution of the Reformation in the history of Western Christendom was not the addition of new doctrines, but the personalization of the whole content of doctrine. Christian faith which for centuries had been an objective entity, a series of revealed doctrines (in the plural) was now in all its aspects understood as a relational entity, the encounter between a gracious God and a lost sinner. The plurality of truths was now understood as the expression of this one truth; or as Calvin said: as the knowledge of the divine goodness to us.[2]

We will now enumerate some major features of the faith-concept which was so central to this new discovery:

1. We have mentioned already the basic element of *personalization*. We must never lose sight of this, lest we misunderstand what faith is. The revealing, promising, forgiving God in his condescension meets man in an extremely unequal encounter. God is revealing, man is accepting. God is promising, man is believing. God is forgiving, man is responding in humble gratitude.

2. Therefore, *Word and faith belong together*. Faith is knowledge (*cognitio*) of the word, which is more than knowledge, it is acknowledgement, recognition (*notitia*) and *assensus* in one. Faith points always away from itself, it is not interested in itself, only in the word which it bears and gladly accepts. It can as little be separated and observed apart from its object, the promises of God, as the rays from the sun. We must never forget, as Calvin says, that the relationship of faith to the word is permanent and it can no more be separated from the word than the rays from the sun whence they originate. And 'take away the word and no faith will remain'.[3]

3. Though faith is the other end of a personal relation, this does not mean that man can believe by his own insight and power. God himself must grant him the gift of illumination. Calvin said that this knowledge (*cognitio*) is revealed and sealed by the *Holy Spirit*. This is also a common conviction of the Reformation, but not a new one. The Council of Orange (529) had already pronounced it powerfully in its series of 'canons concerning grace' (*canones de gratia*).

4. Faith is one unified existential act. Nevertheless the Reformers distinguish in this one act two sides, two aspects. Calvin uses for the oneness, the word *cognitio*, and then distinguishes between a revelation in the mind and a sealing in the hearts. This distinction within the *cognitio* shows that this term is not meant in a mere intellectual sense, but rather as the equivalent of the Old Testament verb *jada* and the noun *da'at*. The knowledge of the Lord means: living in his communion,

having experience of his gracious disposition towards us. But to express this faith-reality we need two words: revelation and sealing (*obsignatio*). This latter goes deeper than the first, into the very core of existence, to the heart itself (*in cor ipsum*), where it creates security (*securitas*), confidence (*fiducia*). So faith has two elements: knowledge and confidence, in this order. Knowledge is the root, confidence is the fruit. For confidence we must first know whom or what we can trust. And knowledge of the benevolence of God which is not followed by confidence, is no real knowledge, but an outward *fides historica*, which is a contradition in itself. Faith and confidence (*fides* and *fiducial*) belong together.

5. As a consequence of it, faith for the Reformers implied *securitas*, full conviction about one's personal salvation. That is why Calvin speaks of a 'firm and certain knowledge' '*firmam certamque cognitionem*'. He and his partisans become eloquent when they show how indissolubly this element belongs to the real act of faith, just as in a marriage, mutual love implies the conviction that divorce is impossible. Only the neutral observer leaves room for doubt.

6. As we see, the one act of faithful surrender implies the different elements which in Scholastic thinking were spread over separate notions. We must yet point to two indissoluble elements in which faith unfolds itself; *mortificatio* and *vivificatio*. Faith starts a process in man in which the old self dies more and more while a new self is born. In these words of the Heidelberg Catechism: on the one hand 'sincere sorrow over our sins and more and more to hate them and to flee from them', and on the other hand, 'complete joy in God through Christ and a strong desire to live according to the will of God in all good works' (answers 89 and 90). For this reason faith means a constant *struggle*. And not for this reason only but also because we are constantly inclined neither to believe nor to trust the promises of God. Therefore Calvin says, 'for the faithful there is a continual battle against their own lack of confidence'.[4] Or as Luther said: 'Faith is a restless thing.'

7. Where faith is such an all-embracing concept, it would be understandable that the Reformers would consider love, hope

and the life of renewal as mere elements and aspects of the fgith. What we indicated about *mortificatio* and *vivificatio* points in that direction. In general Luther is more inclined to stress the unity of all these aspects within the one faith, whereas Calvin sometimes distinguishes between faith itself and its immediate consequences such as confidence, certainty, hope. But both keep to the Pauline triad: faith-hope-love. They differ from Scholasticism in that they refuse to consider *love* as a higher virtue apart from faith, which imparts to faith its effectiveness. On the contrary, as Calvin says: 'It is faith alone which first begets charity in us'.[5] Love is the direct consequence of faith, flowing from faith as the river from the source. Faith works through love (*Gal.* 5:6) and love is the reverse of faith.

8. A difficult point for other believers to understand is how, in faith, *passivity and activity*, instrumentality and creativity, go together. On the one hand faith is nothing in itself. It is not meritorious, it is not a condition for entering into salvation. Christ alone saves, not faith. Faith is, as Flacius puts it, not more than the '*manus mendica*', the hand which the beggar holds up to receive the gift. The '*fiat*' of faith is (as that of Mary was), not creative nor co-operative nor complementary, but purely instrumental. But as such it is indispensable and even constitutive, and on account of its mere instrumentality, it is even a source of creativity, the canal through which the divine forces of renewal flow into life. As Luther put it: in the surrender of faith we abandon our false gods; by that we fulfil the first commandment, and by implication we then fulfil all the commandments. Probably in our modern times we can better understand and express these deep insights. Only a man who is radically freed from all spasmodic efforts to maintain and to justify himself, is free for creative love towards his surroundings. Therefore to the much heard objection against the Reformers' concept of faith: 'Does not this teaching make people careless and sinful?' the only answer is that given by the Heidelberg Catechism (64): 'No, for it is impossible for those who are ingrafted into Christ by true faith not to bring forth the fruit of gratitude.'

We conclude this first section with a short word about the concept of faith in the Council of Trent. This concept is found in the Decree on Justification and was meant as the official Catholic answer to the Reformation concept. For the sake of brevity, I quote only the central and characteristic Canon 77:

> If anyone shall say that men are justified either by the sole imputation of the justice of Christ or by the sole remission of sins, to the exclusion of the grace and the charity that is poured forth in their hearts by the Holy Spirit and remains in them, or also that the grace by which we are justified is only the good will of God: a. s.[6]

The first half of the condemned sentence would be rejected by the Reformers as well. Instead of '*exclusa*' they taught: '*inclusa*'. But therefore they would reject the latter part and reply: 'What more can grace be than the favour of God? Do we need more? Does not the relation with this favour include a radical renewal?' We see that here two modes of thinking clash. One is that of the scholastic tradition with its objectivistic and substantialistic thinking. The other is that of thinking in terms of encounter, relation, personalization. The first thought in the either-or of *extrinsecus* and *instrinsecus*: grace is a power which is either in you or not in you. The latter occurred in a climate in which the philosophical language was not yet available. What happens in a personal encounter is neither *extrinsecus* nor *instrinsecus*. But for lack of the necessary philosophical tools Reformers had often to use in the debates the terminology of the opponents and to express their insights in terms of extrinsecism. It was not until the twentieth century that the reality of personal encounter found an adequate philosophical expression. Now the debate about the role and content of faith can be taken up again. And even more so because the Council of Trent, in spite of its inclination to a 'Jacobean' concept of faith (*Jas.* 2:17 ff.) instead of a Pauline one, expressed in different chapters of the Decree essential biblical insights which kept the door ajar for better times. I think especially of Chapter 8, in which faith is not only called the beginning (*initium*) but also the foundation and the root of all justification (*fundamentum ex radix omnis justificationis*), words which cannot be misunderstood as if faith itself would be the justifying work, because the *causae iustificationis* are mentioned in the chapter before.

Objectivization and Interiorization

According to a historically doubtful story Luther is reported to have said shortly before his death: 'This doctrine will be obscured after my time.' If it be not true, it is well invented.[7] After the shock and excitement of the liberating discoveries, of the great Reformers, a second generation grew up for which the pure doctrine was more or less self-evident and which in its struggle with the Counter-Reformation was in need of a more explicit and theoretical reflection. Now the lack of adequate philosophical categories made itself keenly perceptible. Small wonder that the polemical theologians of the Reformation tried to refute their opponents, in the first place the formidable Jesuit Bellarmine, by using the same intellectual armour, i.e. scholastic categories and distinctions. This inclination is observable as early as in Luther's collaborator Melanchthon. Especially after 1560 this trend rapidly wins ground. In order to understand what this means for our subject, let me quote one of the most famous pronouncements about faith in the Reformed tradition, the 21st question and answer of the *Heidelberg Catechism*. (This catechism was published in 1563, just on the border-line of the two epochs, mainly written by Ursinus, a follower of Bullinger, Calvin and Melanchthon.)

> What is true faith? It is not only a certain knowledge by which I accept as true all that God has revealed to us in his Word, but also a wholehearted trust which the Holy Spirit creates in me through the Gospel, that not only to others but to me also God has given the forgiveness of sins, everlasting righteousness and salvation, out of sheer grace solely for the sake of Christ's saving work.

An excellent confession; nevertheless with some big snakes in the grass:

(*a*) Unlike Calvin's formulation, the two elements of faith are no longer subsumed under a master-concept like *cognitio*. Linked by a 'not only—but also', *assensus* and *fiducia* are treated as separate categories.

(*b*) This is related to the fact that knowledge is conceived here slightly but importantly differently from the way Calvin conceived it. For Calvin the object was God's benevolence in Christ. He agreed with his opponent Pighius that there is more revealed to us, e.g. the commandments of the Law and God's wrath and judgement. They form together the general object of faith (*generale fidei objectum*). But what really distinguishes the faithful from the others is their surrender to God's mercy. 'The state of faith will not be secure unless it is grounded in the mercy of God.'[8] The same was even more strongly said by Luther; he accepted in the Bible as object of faith only what promotes Christ (*was Christum treibet*). In the Heidelberg Catechism, however, the object of faith is: 'all that God has revealed to us in his Word.' With this change in the object, faith itself changes also. It becomes now a more or less impersonal *acceptance of supernatural truths* which may or may not go together with an existential engagement. Structurally faith is here quite similar to the historical faith (*fides historica*) so vehemently rejected by the Reformers of the first generation.

(*c*) As a logical consequence of this, the element of confidence (*fiducia*) now stands more or less *in opposition to that of assent* (*assensus*). The *assensus* is general and intellectual. The *fiducia* is personal and existential. And, which is very remarkable, the act of faith is no longer, as a whole, created by the Holy Spirit. It is only 'a wholehearted trust which the Holy Spirit creates in me'. Here a serious split in the concept of faith emerges, though the composers of the catechism were hardly aware of it and tried in the formulation to do justice to the unity of both elements.

Nevertheless, there are now two separate elements, each of which developed in its own way. The assensus concept led to a staunch *orthodoxy* which carried on an endless controversy with its Catholic opponents about the question whether we have to believe the revealed truths because they are written in the infallible Bible or because they are taught by the infallible Church. On this line the Protestant Church members were educated in an objectivistic intellectualistic scholastic faith.

Many serious Christians, however, deplored what they called an outward and dead faith. They accepted this objectivism as one half of the faith, but they wanted to see it *complemented by the personal assurance* of which the second part of the definition in the Heidelberg Catechism spoke. Shortly after 1600, different movements, inspired by the ideal of a more personal and internal faith, came into being, in several countries (England, the Netherlands, Scotland, Germany) under several names (Pietism, Neaner Reformation, later on also Methodism). They all took the content of the Protestant faith for granted. Their problem was 'How do I know that I am a true believer? that I am really converted? that I have in my life the evidence of my election?' The Reformers said: 'Turn away from your sinful "I"; surrender to Christ.' Now in the new process of internalization the question is: 'Though I believe the whole Bible, how do I know that the Spirit really turned me away from myself and that I am now a child of God?' Faith is now no longer an act to be performed, but a new habit to be investigated and stated. As early as 1619 the Canons of the Synod of Dordrecht had anticipated this development in the words: 'The elect become assured of their eternal and irrevocable election . . . when they in themselves observe with a spiritual joy and holy delight the infallible fruits of election indicated in the Word of God, i.e., true faith in Christ, childlike fear of God, godly grief about sin, hunger and thirst for righteousness, and so on' (1, 12). The concept of relation, of person-to-person meeting, has broken down and has been replaced by the complementary concepts of *externalization and internalization*, of objectivism and subjectivism, of Scholasticism and mysticism. One wonders where precisely lay the difference from the traditional Catholic position. On both sides assent and confidence (*assensus et fiducia*), mind and will, are separated; historical faith (*fides historica*) is by both considered as the initial stage, which has to be superseded by personal inward application; and personal assurance about one's eternal salvation is on both sides the rare fruit of a special revelation. As we can understand there were intimate connections between Catholic mysticism and Protestant pietism in the seventeenth century.

This far too brief exposition would, however, be incomplete

and even distorted, were we not to add that beneath this theological surface and also in some theologians, in various kinds of teaching, preaching, pastoral care and personal belief, the new approach and synthesis of the Reformers was kept alive. Let me mention only one (late) example, the famous Dutch-German preacher, H. F. Kohlbrugge, who was engaged in the middle of the nineteenth century in a constant struggle with pietistic introversion, for whom faith meant a radical turning away from one's sins and one's piety, from one's signs of grace and one's lack of signs, and who defined faith as: 'taking God for a man of his word'.

Naturalization and Subjectivization

In the meantime the secularization of Western culture made rapid progress. Man with his reason and experience became more and more the measure of all things. Pietism was from this point of view a more modern phenomenon than scholastic orthodoxy both in its Catholic and Protestant forms. Room for an intellectual authoritarian system about an unverifiable supernatural world only acceptable through a '*sacrificium intellectus*' became increasingly more narrow. The assent to a revelation, for centuries taken for granted, became more and more problematic. In the opinion of intellectuals up to the present day, Kant gave it its death-blow. He stated that the access to 'reality itself' and so to any supernatural world, was debarred to our pure reason which with its categories is only valid in the field of our horizontal experience. At the same time Kant opened another entrance: practical reason with its categorical imperative must necessarily make postulates about the existence of a God as the maintainer of the moral law. So for Kant faith was the result of our moral nature. Many theologians did not follow him in his solution, but the majority of the leading Protestant theologians accepted his starting-point that faith does not belong to the realm of reason and therefore is not, at least, primarily, a *cognitio*, *notitia* or *assensus*. They wrestled with the problem: *to what realm then does faith belong?* The putting of this question is typical of much of the theology of the nineteenth and twentieth centuries. The question is even more typical than the various answers are, because it implies suppositions which must necessarily drastically limit the possible answers. The two main suppositions may be stated thus: 1. Faith is a function of man's nature; it is rooted in a faculty of man's mind and can therefore, if rightly phrased, be made more or less acceptable to the general mind. 2. It follows that this faculty of man's mind is, if not the source of religion and revelation, at least the standard according to which the acceptability of revelation is to be judged. These two suppositions I call the *naturalization* and the *subjectivization* of faith. Clearly, we are here far away from the concept of faith of the Reformers. These theologians are hardly interested in notions of faith as a gift of the Holy Spirit, conversion, the scandal of faith. But they are concerned with the challenge of the modern mind, of which the Reformers in their *Christiana tempora* were only dimly aware, and they are prepared to meet the new challenge.

As two great examples of this attitude in the nineteenth century I mention Schleiermacher and Ritschl. Schleiermacher did not seek the entrance to the world of faith in the moral field. He believed that faith, as he called it, is 'a distinct province in man's existence'. It is the awareness of man's absolute dependence. This awareness is constantly suppressed by our sin, but kept alive in communion with Christ through the Church. What we usually call the content of faith is a series of consequences concerning God, ourself and the world, derived from this awareness of absolute dependence. Schleiermacher offers us a most pure and radical form of the post-Kantian theological approach—too radical for many, who felt that the nature of faith as a response to an encounter with the Word of a personal God was absent in this concept.

Differing from Schleiermacher, Ritschl keeps closer to Kant. For him faith has to do with the moral realm of life. Man in his moral struggle, i.e. in his striving for personality and for dominance over nature, is supported and directed by Jesus Christ, by his faithfulness to his vocation, his forgiveness of sins, his preaching of the kingdom of God. All these are decisive values for man. They bring him to value pronouncements about Jesus as the Son of God, about reconciliation, consummation etc. These pronouncements are secondary in relation to the value-experience, which is the authentic experience of faith. The element of knowledge is minimized in favour of the element of confidence.

The two examples which I take from our own century point in the same direction. The first and great example is Bultmann. For him faith is the act by which man realizes his existence. Each man is called to exist, to stand out from the world, as a real self. But sin prevents man from realizing his authenticity. Only the message of the crucified Christ has the power to make man follow his real vocation. So faith is a decision, an act of obedience. In this act God, the proclamation (kerygma), the crucified Christ, are meaningful to me. They form a more or less objective counter-element to me, which helps me to establish my existence. They are the God-given means which help man to attain his end: a life of authentic existence.

The last theologian whom I mention in this connection is Bultmann's former student, Ebeling, one of the so-called neo- or post-Bultmannians. I mention him because so far as I see he is the only theologian who has the category of faith (in the sense of *fides qua creditur*[9] at the very centre of his theology. But it is not easy to make his position clear in a few words. He sees man as created for an encounter through words. But so often words do not meet man's need. Man knows in his conscience about God and what he knows frightens him. But Jesus through his life and death appeals to the God of omnipotent love, who rescues us from anxiety. God has heard him and raised him from the dead. Now he, the true witness of faith, becomes to us the ground of faith. He is the Word-event in which God is present and which meets the distress of our conscience. This meeting is the creation of faith; and faith is the goal of the Word-event, because in the act of believing against his anxiety man becomes real man. This sounds like Bultmann, but the element of encounter is far clearer here. However, the nature of the Word-event and its relation to God and Christ are somewhat obscure. The starting-point in existentialist naturalism and subjectivism prevents Ebeling from putting the Word at the beginning and in the centre, as the Reformers did. In the centre is man's act of faith as an act of confidence, encouraged by an encountering Word-event.

All these (German) theologians *appeal to Luther* and to his emphasis on the element of personal trust. Unlike Luther and the other Reformers, however, these post-Kantians treat the objective role in the encounter and therefore also the element of *motitia* as secondary. The whole trend of the Reformation concept of faith is reversed in the direction of the human subject.

And what can we report about the Catholic position in this post-Kantian epoch? In the year 1870, when Ritschl was at his culminating-point, the First Vatican Council proclaimed: 'And the Catholic Church teaches that this faith, which is the beginning of man's salvation, is a supernatural virtue whereby, inspired and assisted by the grace of God, we believe that the things which he has revealed are true . . .'[10] Here nothing has changed since the *Sententiae* of Petrus Lombardus. The word 'beginning' (*initium*) taken from the baptismal liturgy, is maintained; the two other words which Trent added—'foundation and root' (*fundamentum et radix*)—are left out. Whereas in the Protestant theology of that time the personal and empirical character of faith was one-sidedly emphasized, the Catholic Council, just as one-sidedly as its opponents, stressed its initial, intellectual and supernatural aspects. For one thing the object of faith is an existential singular, for the other it is an intellectual plurality. Here the two confessions were much further removed from one another than in the time of Trent.

We must not forget, however, that the Reformation concept of faith was preserved beneath the surface of academic theology in Churches, groups and individuals everywhere. Even many theologians in the nineteenth century tried to maintain it, though they often weakened their position in that they, as well as their opponents, tried as much as possible to develop the act and the content of faith on the basis of the human subject.

Barth was not the first to see that weakness, but he was the most radical in making a Copernican revolution. He started no longer with man and his needs, but God and his Word. So he returned to the position of the Reformers and restored the responding re-acting, referring character of faith, without forgoing its existential, '*confidentia*' character. It is understandable that in his two larger expositions of the nature of faith (*Church Dogmatics*

1, i and IV, i) he, like Calvin, characterizes faith primarily as knowledge (*cognitio*), as acknowledgement (*Anerkennung*)—a comprehensive word which in his thinking embraces all other aspects such as confidence, obedience etc. Barth was the main but by no means the only thinker prominent in the revival of the Reformation concept of faith after the First World War. Two elements contributed strongly to this turn in official theology: firstly, the new flourishing of biblical theology, which made it perfectly clear that the New Testament word '*pistis*' always refers to a transcendent Word-reality and means acceptance and confidence in one; secondly the new phenomenological philosophy which found man's nature in dialogue, in the I-Thou relation, in being met from outside; this new approach helped to clarify positions and in the long run also influenced the ecumenical situation, as we shall see.

Some aspects of the present situation

In these years the act of faith is not a central theme in Protestant theology. The cultural winds have shifted from idealism to empiricism. We are now less interested in the human subject of experience than in the verifiable contents of experience. The interest in the *fides qua* has given way to a new interest in the *fides quae creditur*. But we cannot separate them. And one interest has remained, just because of the new shift to empiricism: the quest for establishing faith in man's common nature, what we called the naturalization of faith.

In many circles Barth's theology of the Word and therefore also his concept of faith still prevail. There is a tendency among his younger adherents to relate this concept more than the master did, to man's ordinary experience and to what Tillich called 'his search for ultimate truth'. In other circles the approach of Bultmann is still dominant, but among his followers we notice the tendency (as we saw in Ebeling) not to put the concept of (subjective) existence in the centre, but that of encounter with the Word-event. So there are convergent lines on both sides. And because of the tendency of naturalization, there is also a convergence (partly due to Tillich) towards the Catholic concept of faith as related to man's self-transcendence (Rahner). Heinrich

Ott's book, *Der personliche Gott* (1969), is an expression of these convergencies.

A most daring example of the will to prove the natural character —and even the rationality—of faith is offered by Wolfhart Pannenberg. He rejects any idea of a *sacrificium intellectus*. The content of faith as knowledge about historical facts is accessible and provable to everyone. There is no supernatural knowledge. It is basically possible for historical research to discover the truth of the Resurrection, of revelation, of Jesus as God and man, etc. Faith depends on historical knowledge, it presupposes a special field of generally accessible knowledge. In itself it is not knowledge, but the firm confidence that this history has saving significance for me and that the God who raised Jesus from the dead will finally overcome. This is a highly remarkable and exceptional position. Pannenberg puts and answers the difficult and often evaded question about the dependence of faith on the historical-critical research. But this answer is at the cost of the unity between *notitia* and *fiducia* in the one act of faith.

More influential both in Catholic and in Protestant theological circles is the concept of faith offered by Jergen Moltmann in his book *Theology of Hope* (1964) and many other publications. To put it briefly: for Moltmann faith is almost identical with hope; in faith we anticipate the 'not yet', the 'Utopia', the future of God as promised to us in the resurrection of Jesus. In this theology the reference of faith to the past of Christ and the present of the Spirit is underestimated in favour of the reference to the future. Nevertheless this is a wholesome shift to a much neglected aspect. We should not forget that in Hebrews faith is mainly conceived in this way and is even defined as 'the ground of things hoped for' (11:1). We might say that the traditional Catholic concept of faith is Jacobean, that the classical Protestant concept is Pauline and that probably a common interest in the third New Testament type, that of Hebrews, can bring the confessions nearer to one another on this point.

This leads us to the last point, but by no means the least important, that of the present agreement and disagreement between Catholics and Protestants with regard to the concept of faith. We may say that we are at the moment far nearer to one

another than a century ago in the time of Ritschl and Vatican I.
We may even say that we never were so near to one another on
this point. This is mainly due to the already mentioned twofold
influence, that of biblical theology and that of phenomenological
philosophy, both of which made a deep impact first on Protestant
theology, but after the Second World War made a probably
deeper impact on Catholic theology. It would be easy to quote a
large number of Catholic theologians who describe the act of
faith in a way which hardly differs from that of Reformed
theology. However, I limit myself here to three utterances of a
less private nature.

The first is the Constitution on Divine Revelation (1965) of
Vatican II which in article 5 described faith as 'an obedience by
which man entrusts his whole self freely to God, offering "the
full submission of intellect and will to God who reveals", and
freely assenting to the truth revealed by him'. We notice that
here faith is an act of man as a whole and that its object is not a
plurality of truths, but God himself and truth in the singular.
The Abbot-Gallagher edition of the Vatican Documents adds in
a note: 'The Council desired to get away from a too intellectualist
conception. Christian faith is not merely assent to a set of statements; it is a personal engagement, a continuing act of loyalty
and self-commitment, offered by man to God.'[11]

The second document I quote is the Dutch *New Catechism*.
It relates faith to conscience and compares it with faith in the
partner in a marriage. The opening words of the section read:
'The Gospel show Jesus speaking more frequently of faith than
of love. Faith is the gift of the Spirit which enables us to give
ourselves entirely to him who is greater than we, and to accept
his message. Faith does not consist of mere reasoning.' And
further on we read: 'Faith is a leap, but not an irresponsible one.
It is justified by the leap itself.'[12]

The third quotation is from the article 'Faith' in Rahner and
Vorgrimler's *Concise Theological Dictionary*. The Introduction
points out that in faith we almost always have to do with 'a
relationship between persons'. Accordingly, 'God's disclosure to
the human person is not mere intellectual information'; it
'appeals to all the dimensions of man so as to order them all to

God', so that faith 'in its complete fulfilment is love'.[13]

This does not mean that all disagreements are removed. The Dutch *New Catechism* sees as a difficulty which still remains the fact that 'It is a typically Catholic perspective to see faith and reason as related to each other' while 'the Reformation with its constant attitude of reserve towards the salvific possibilities of the earthly, emphasizes the otherness of faith'.[14] Here a difference yet remains. However, after what we have seen about the ongoing process since Kant to discover the roots of faith in the human mind, at least in an important part of Protestant theology, it is hard to say how significant this difference is.

I feel more disagreement when I read in the Dictionary of Rahner and Vorgrimler the article on 'fiducial faith' as the typical Protestant concept of faith. The article states that the difference at the present is almost exclusively a terminological one, also 'that faith which attains the complete fulfilment of its nature in total self-surrender to God is that charity which justifies faith'. In sentences like these I still hear the inclination to distinguish between faith and love and to relate them as the lower and the higher stage of a process. The Reformation is inclined to avoid process language in this realm, and when it uses it (as the Augustinian Calvin frequently does), it means a process in which faith controls more and more (Calvin's beloved *magis ac magis*) man's heart, deeds and emotions; faith and love always grow together, because love is the direct expression and reverse of faith.

To my mind, however, our remaining disagreements lie more in the context in which faith functions, especially the context of Scriptures, tradition and Church, and their mutual relations. To put it briefly: the role of the Church in faith is so different that for the Catholic faith it is primarily a communal act and for the Protestant a personal act. Now personal and communal do not exclude one another; they are even complementary. But what is true in biblical faith and in theology, is far from yet being true in our practice. What the Catholic calls communal is often to a Protestant view, collectivism; and what the Protestant calls personal is often in the view of the Catholic, individualism.

The Historical Church as Mediator of Faith

JAMES P. MACKEY

'I BELIEVE in . . . one, holy, Catholic and apostolic Church.' We shall have something to say later about the word 'historical' in the title of this paper. We shall have to ask if the Church is historical in every sense; if it is not sometimes, or in some senses, a-historical.

But first let us remark simply that the theologian who sets out to discover the relationship between the Church and faith, is likely to be thrown at the very beginning of the course by the apparent attempt, in many forms of the creed, to make the Church itself an object of faith. He will remember Aquinas' insistence that God is not only the formal object of faith, the one in whom we believe, but also the only principal referent of the material object of faith, that is to say, though we make mention of other things in outlining the content of *the faith*, we may never give the impression that any of them are objects of faith in their own right. We may only mention them as elements in our relationship to God, the goal of our existence.[1]

In his *Early Christian Creeds*, Kelly remarked that the lumping together at the end of the old Roman Creed of such disparate subjects as Church, forgiveness of sins, resurrection of the flesh, with the Holy Spirit, all under the rubric 'I believe in', caused considerable embarrassment to more sophisticated Trinitarian theologians of the fourth century.[2] But though the impression of a laundry-bag collection conveyed by these endings of the creeds can be embarrassing, the logic of the additions is obvious enough and could be accepted by Aquinas: it does not mean that any of the additions is made an object of faith in its own right.

Only God is an object of religious faith in his own right.

It is clear from the New Testament that the Spirit of God works to add new members continually to the community, that men are forgiven, raised from the dead even, by the Spirit or power of God. So, in these apparently rag-tag-and-bobtail endings of the creeds we are still professing faith in God and in nothing and no one else. We profess to believe that the Spirit of God sending men to preach and confirm those who hear them is constantly adding to the Church, the people of God. We believe that he forgives us our sins, we believe and hope that he will defeat for us even death, the last enemy, which we cannot at all hope to defeat ourselves. We do not profess belief in the Church as an object entirely distinct from God, as an agent additional to God. That would be blasphemy. The Church results from the gathering of men of faith, made possible by God, men of faith whose witness can contribute to the evocation of faith in other men, a faith also made possible by God. So, then, the Church is not an object of religious faith in its own right; but only as a result of God's action on men, God who alone is an object of religious faith in his own right. In the endings of the creeds when we mention the Church, as when we mention forgiveness and resurrection, we are professing belief in God, his actions, their efficacy.

But because the Church is not an object of faith in its own right, does this mean that we can go to something of an opposite extreme and look on it as a human phenomenon—a society of men of faith, yes, but still a society of men which can be questioned about its effect on the faith of men, either its own individual members or others? Can we look on the Church as a society of men with its verifiable structure and constitution, its professed beliefs and perceptible practices? Can we look on it as a human institution acting out its part on the stage of history, and can we ask the question: what does the Church, looked on from this external point of view, have to do with the faith of men? Such a way of looking at the Church, such a question, might seem odd to many people, and even objectionable to some. The Church, they would say, is the mother who begot you in faith, or begot faith in you. How can you than ask: what has the Church to do with the faith of men? As if you could find faith apart from the Church and then, from your independent standpoint, discuss the Church's role *vis-à-vis* faith.

We must make some distinctions here. Faith for me as for every man is a possibility which grows out of my perception of the quality of my own existence and of the existence of my world. Certain particular events may help to specify the content of this faith for me, may help inform me more specifically, that is, about the God I am dependent on, the more precise nature of my relationship with him, the hope which this relationship holds out, and so on. Or certain people may read events in a special way that will then recommend itself to me. Certain men may even claim special experiences in connection with a particular historical event, which would enable them to interpret it in a special way. (This happened, in the case of the so-called Christ-event for those who claimed to be witnesses of the resurrection-appearances.) But all this testimony must be seen as a specification of my basic faith, not a purely extrinsic addition to it. For only as such, as specification, indeed perhaps definitive specification, am I enabled to assess and to accept it as my own faith.

The Christian Churches are the communities of those who have accepted the specifications of man's basic faith brought about by the teaching, the life and the destiny of Jesus of Nazareth, by the interpretations given this by certain privileged individuals.

History, however, did not end with the Christ-event; nor did man's capacity, in imitation of the special genius of Israel, for looking to history rather than to the cosmos as such, for a more specific indication of the nature of God and of his relationship to mankind. Nor did the differences cease in the ways of expressing the content of this faith—differences that depended on changes in the historical circumstances themselves or on the mentality of the interpreter. If the earlier Paul was convinced of the imminence of the *Eschaton*, the sheer historical circumstance of its delay soon forced him and other New Testament writers to see more significance in the Christ-event for life in this present world, thus changing somewhat their expression of the content of *the faith*. The more apocalyptic-type thinker is always inclined to see the present in terms of purgative suffering from which

men can only hope to escape by a gracious and definitive intervention of God. This type of thinker arises usually in historical
circumstances of persistent tribulation. Others, even in times of
tribulation, are, like the propher Jeremiah, still capable of
believing that men can turn to God and thus hope for a bettering
of their present history in this world, beyond the punishment of
their present tribulations. These are examples of changes in
historical circumstances and in the mentalities of men resulting
in changes in expression of the content of the faith. But there is
also development in man's consciousness of himself, his world,
his history, and this too means development in man's religious
consciousness and in the content of his faith. In more primitive
times, when man is not so conscious of his individual worth,
when the individual is submerged in the tribe, and history is
history only of the tribe, man's ideas of God and of God's dealings
can be morally crude. As his consciousness of himself and of his
history develops this moral crudeness in his religious consciousness gradually disappears. Much in the Old Testament illustrates
this. Man's consciousness of his world also dictates his ideas of
God and God's action, ordering, creating, conserving, guiding.
When man's consciousness of the world is restricted to physical
impressions of land and sea and plants and animals, when the
stars are lights hanging in the dome of the sky, God is the great
arranger. Later God can be a cosmic mover, later still a true
Creator, then perhaps an Omega point to an evolving universe.
Man's religious consciousness develops with development in his
consciousness of himself, his history, his world—and this too
results in differences in his expression of the content of his faith.

Because of this third source of change or difference in the
content of men's faith it is doubtful if man nowadays could use
any of the Old Testament ways of interpreting historical events,
could simply transpose those methods of interpretation to current
events of the recent past. If we can no longer in this evolution-
conscious age use the Greek concept of the Logos-God, the
eternal and immutable exemplar of a basically static universe, if
we do not even know how God guides evolution (since we don't
know the laws of evolution, for one thing, and, for another, we
are beginning to realize that we must be as agnostic about God's

action as traditional thought has always told us we must be about his nature), neither can we say in any direct fashion any longer that he causes this or that historical event—the rise or fall of a people. We are much more conscious that the future of history and of evolution is increasingly in our own hands, and our misfortunes are much more our own shortcomings and failures coming against us. In addition, because we are so much more conscious of our own responsibility for the fate of the world and of mankind, we are less inclined than our predecessors to think or talk apocalyptically—that is, to think and talk in terms that convey an impression of another world and another life radically different from, radically discontinuous with this one. But the Christian specification of a basic faith in God as Lord of the world and of history, a specification which we believe to be definitive, leads us to accept an absolute claim, that is a claim of God, on our obedience in caring for our brother in the present concrete conditions of this world and this history; and it leads us at the same time to an absolute trust that God will vindicate us even beyond death, though we may not know how continuity with our present history can then be maintained. Such a claim, such a trust certainly were characteristic of the mission and destiny of Jesus.

Faith then, is by no means a static thing. According to the special genius of the Judaeo-Christian tradition, it is a commitment to a God who is attained through the concrete conditions of this life, a commitment concretely expressed in one's spiritual and practical reaction to the concrete conditions of life. It undergoes change, then, in accordance with differing historical circumstances, differing mentalities amongst believers, and development in man's consciousness of himself and his total environment, while remaining the same as man's most basic relationship to God, while remaining Christian by giving specifically Christian form to man's basic relationship to God through all these changes. Faith is a commitment that is invited and must be re-made in the concrete circumstances of each different day. Christian faith is a following-of-Christ-type response that is invited and must be re-made in the concrete circumstances of each different day.

Faith is an intensely individual and personal affair. Each man must ask in the integrity of his own heart whether or not he really believes in God—that is whether he really entrusts himself to an ultimate ground of being or not, and then he must ask himself what such entrusting to a ground of being really involves for him. Does it involve trusting that God will make something of this world, or just that he will substitute a better one for this? If the former, does it involve this man's own co-operation, and to what extent? Does it involve trusting that God will still give existence beyond the destruction of his person which we call death? He must ask himself these questions in utter seriousness and answer them for himself. Only the answers he can truly give himself can he offer for possible acceptance by others. It would be totally immoral for any man to offer to others articles of faith which did not in fact correspond to what he believed in his own heart.

Faith is my acknowledgement of God; and its content is derived from what I acknowledge God to be and to do and to be about to do in relationship to me and to my world. As already remarked, I only come upon God in his relationship to me and to my world. There are no articles of faith, no 'things I believe', which have to do entirely with other people or things or events, and which I could therefore offer to others without taking into account my own honest position in belief or unbelief. All articles of faith, since their only principal referent is God, have to do, like God, with the existential contingency of my existence, my life, my future, my world, and I must treat them as such. Otherwise I mistake their nature and my preaching them to others is only leading others astray. For instance, I do not and cannot believe in the resurrection of Jesus except in the context of my own basic acknowledgement of a God who can and may confer life even beyond death. I do not and cannot believe that Jesus' death was for the forgiveness of sins except in the context of my own basic acknowledgement of a God who can and may overlook the backsliding in my own part of the task of building the earth and allow me to return to the task again. All this is also involved in saying that the Christian faith is a specification of basic faith, not a substitution for it or the addition of something totally extrinsic to it. To the extent then, that I do really have Christian faith, I can invite such faith in others and they can respond to me out of their own basic faith. They can accept a God who raises from the dead, who vindicates men, forgiving and restoring them when the blood of the just man, in this case the blood of Jesus, calls to him for vindication. In other words, they can accept the invitation, addressed to them by Christians, to give to a faith that is possible for them in any case, a definitive Christian form.

Ideally speaking the Christian community is simply the gathering of those individuals who make this response, each one in and from his own heart, in and from his own concrete situation amongst others. It is the gathering of those who can try to inform the faith of others, others who also have in principle at least the open possibility of commitment to God and who are also trying to deal with the world and the history that they know—so that these too can recognize from their own spiritual possibilities what the Christians are recommending, as a specification of a commitment that is possible to them also, rather than a suggestion totally strange to them at first, and can as such adopt it.

From this brief analysis, then, three things would follow. First there can be true faith in God outside the Church. Men outside the Church can know what true faith is and so they do have a criterion which will enable them to judge whether what the Christians offer in pronouncement and practice is really a higher specification of their faith or a deterioration of faith. Secondly, the analysis shows that faith is a dynamic affair; whether in Christian or non-Christian form, it is always invited to move with the dynamism of that history which is its source. Lastly, it is an intensely personal affair.

But any gathering of people, probably of necessity, structures itself in a particular way, becomes an institution, centralized to a greater or lesser extent, with a public voice and a public image. There is always the possibility of tension between something which is intensely personal, dynamic and in some basic form independent of a particular society, between this and the public profession and practice of a well-structured society.

Our question then is justified: what has the Church as human institution to do with the faith of men? For an institution with solid structure and public policy can become so engrossed in such structure and policy as to resist the dynamism of change whose real source is the individual believer who in answer to the changes of his historical situation, continually searches his own heart. The Church, acting as institution, *can* lessen the faith of its members and prevent the growth of faith in others; or it can foster the faith of its members and develop in a Christian direction the basic possibilities for faith which exist in all men everywhere.

In order to answer the question: does the Church—looked on now as a society of men with a publicly verifiable structure and constitution, its public profession of beliefs and its particular practices—does the Church looked on in this way help or hinder the faith of men, one would need to pass in review the whole history of the Church and let each age answer for itself. Since there is neither time for this venture nor would I have the necessary expertise to pursue it, let us instead adopt another approach. Instead of talking about the Church through all its historical course, as our title might suggest, let us take instead the Church as we have known it in recent times and know it now, the Church in our own history.

In dealing with the topic of *Tradition and Change in the Church,*[3] I have tried to show how the Christian specification of God's revelation in the world and history (that which newly came in Christ) has to be embodied in the natural and traditional forms of human thought, human institution, human practice (whether particularly symbolic or generally moral), how it has to be handed on, since in its historic specificity it is not repeatable, precisely by being embodied in these cultural forms, how it can only maintain itself by continually re-embodying itself in the continually changing cultural forms of human religions and philosophical thought, human institutions, human patterns of behaviour. Although I know that someone working with more precise historical information than I possessed on the examples I took to illustrate this thesis, or someone aware of changes that have occurred or have been suggested since, would achieve more precise results, still I am convinced that the model I used would now produce similar, if more precise results, and so I have no

intention of repeating that particular theme here. Instead, I want
to turn the theme around. Instead of taking the Christian 'thing',
as Chesterton called it, and trying to see how it became incarnate
in natural and traditional structures, thought categories, moral
and symbolic behaviour patterns in order thus to be propagated
through history and thus to redeem history, let us take some of
the structures, categories and behaviour patterns of our present
culture and ask: are Church structures, thought categories, moral
and symbolic behaviour patterns really now embodied in these,
incarnate in them, so as to be still at this time, a profession and
practice of faith in real history? Or does public Church profession
and practice at this time embody the general cultural patterns,
the general basic faith, of some past time, so that it is unable to
embody the general cultural patterns, the general basic faith of
our time, and so is incapable of Christianizing the men of our
time, of helping and developing their basic faith in the only way
it is commissioned to help and develop this, that is, *by* Christianizing *it*, not some other culture or some past forms of basic
faith.

Let us look at some of the more obvious characteristics of the
general culture and the basic faith of our time.

One word gives the key to man's understanding of the institutions of society in recent and contemporary culture: democracy.
Modern man is only too painfully aware of the shortcomings of
all the democratic systems so far set up in practice—of the graft
and privilege which are so obviously an integral part of their
working. Yet he is convinced of the contribution that each
individual has to make to society, and of the responsibility each
has to exercise. In particular he regards each citizen as responsible
for the choosing of leaders who will then have the authority of
their office to utilize and channel the contributions of each
towards the benefit of all. Modern man will no longer brook the
suggestion that there are lords who rule over him by divine right,
who pass on authority from one to another as a *self-propagating
group*—that is, a group which hands on office either by natural
propagation or by the group itself electing its own replacement.
Such a way of structuring society he considers to belong to an
irrevocable past stage of human culture. He and his likes make

up the people. He will not consider himself a full adult member of the people unless he has a say in what is practised or expressed by the people as a whole, unless in particular he has a direct say in choosing the leaders who will speak and act on behalf of the people. Unless he has, he will consider himself a second-class citizen; he will not regard himself as a member of the people equally with those who presume to rule by right and who therefore bear a responsibility in which he does not substantially share; and nothing will ever really persuade him otherwise. To tell him that he really is equal to all others 'before God' is simply to tell him that he is not really equal at present but that God ignores the present, and has nothing to do with its structure.

One word, also, can give the key to man's understanding of the whole of reality in contemporary culture—evolution. Man is becoming more and more profoundly conscious that the world in which he finds himself has always been and still is, in the making, through that curious process which combines ebb and flow, randomness and apparent direction; and which he knows as evolution. He is aware that history is evolution in its specifically human form—that is to say, that it is the same combination of ebb and flow, randomness and apparent direction, with now the added element of a unique type of randomness, the specifically human element of free creativity. Hence he is aware that his human existence is inescapably historical, in all its facets. In particular he is aware of constant change in his own attempts to understand his evolving self and his evolving world. It is with difficulty that he can find out what the men of previous ages thought; his own prevalent ideas are a constant barrier to this attempt. When he does find out what past men thought he has a contribution to his understanding of reality but not a replacement for it. In short, he is aware of constant change in the content of human concepts and images or, what amounts to the same thing, in the meaning of human words and symbols.

Thomas Aquinas gave us sources of change in moral precept, first, change or development in man's understanding of what is good and what evil and, second, some change in the objective situation in which a moral agent finds himself.[4] The examples which Aquinas used to illustrate his thesis seem almost trite to

modern man precisely because man of this time are so much
aware of how substantially man's understanding of himself, of
what is good or bad for him, can change; and they are also much
more aware of how substantially the objective situation can
change not only for the individual moral agent in his immediate
environment, but for whole populations, for the race as a whole.
Discussion of the legality of warfare in a nuclear age takes place
in a totally different objective situation from that of a pre-nuclear
age. Discussion of the morality of contraception in an over-
populated country or city takes place in a radically different
objective situation from that of an Irish countryside of dwindling
population. From modern man's point of view, it would be
irresponsible, objectively immoral even, of the formulator of
moral precepts to ignore either changes in human insight or
changes in the objective situation in which man finds himself,
the two sources of mutability in moral law which Aquinas
himself pin-pointed.

Finally, one might mention a common clamour amongst the
people of our time that the roles they play or the gesture they are
asked to make, be meaningful, so that they can become actively
involved in a comprehending and, therefore, truly personal
manner. Admittedly this call for meaningfulness can be a pretty
mindless one by dint of sheer repetition; it can sometimes amount
to no more than a desire for the latest fad, the latest catch-word,
the latest behaviour pattern, to have 'caught on'. But in itself it
answers to man's consciousness of his own individual dignity
and to his sense of personal responsibility for his own contribution
and for the reality to which he makes this contribution.

The Church will always be mediator of faith while, as the
people of God, it can be seen to exist as a community of men
and women who do truly believe in God. It will be mediator of
Christian faith to the precise extent that it is seen to be a community of men and women attempting to reach the nature of
Christ in the total commitment of their faith, their total dedica-
tion to the needs of the neighbour, near or far, and their trust that
God will give them, earthly followers of Christ, a future like
Christ's beyond death. The Church will always be mediator of
faith to the precise extent that it is seen to be a community of

men and women who respond to God, in the spirit of Christ, precisely as lords of *this* history and *this* world that they know— that is to say, to the extent that they commit themselves in word and action to this present world as they now understand it at this point of time, as their basic link with God. Such witness, whether in private lives of Christian men and women, or in public acts and pronouncements of Christian bodies, can call forth the faith that is possible for every member of contemporary humanity, and can even form this into a Christian faith.

But suppose that the fact comes home to contemporary man, whether inside or outside the Church, that he is dealing with lordships, and furthermore that they form a self-propagating group, so that he has no say whatever in electing individuals to membership of this group (though apparently Franco has). Suppose in addition that he has some suspicion of the fact that neither the cultural form of lordship nor the self-propagating method of replacement can claim complete historical continuity back to the person of Jesus himself. Suppose he is told that it would be intolerable for anyone 'to want to modify the formulas with which the Council of Trent has proposed the eucharistic mystery for belief', that 'these formulas, and others too which the Church employs in proposing dogmas of faith, express concepts which are not tied to any specific cultural system', that these concepts 'present the perception which the human mind acquires from its universal, essential experience of reality and expresses by use of appropriate and certain terms borrowed from colloquial or literary language', that 'they are, therefore, within the reach of everyone at all times and in all places'.[5] Suppose he is given the impression that the content of the faith, the who and what men are enabled to commit themselves to, can be expressed in concepts and language that are unchangeable, with philosophical or cosmological or psychological or even historical presuppositions that are of immutable validity for all ages . . .

In my earlier paper I said that the word 'faith' can be used, as it is in Scripture, for *the faith*, that is to say, the body of formulated beliefs, formulated always by men, not by God. Now, in the conditions just described, the faith, understood in this sense of a set of human formulations, is bound to take priority over faith. It is bound to seem like a body of truth independent of the course of history and therefore not affecting history. It is bound to seem something *not* attainable either from man's normal experience of the world in his own historical circum-stances, or as a specification of the faith so attained which everyman, not just chosen experts, can understand as specification and hand on or recommend to others as such. It is bound to seem the particular possession of a certain group, thus confirming their lordship and justifying their self-propagation process. The prospective subject of the message preached then finds himself related to a social structure which does not answer to his actual historical experience of society at all (and therefore has only the most indirect effect on his social life, if any at all), through assent to a set of ideas and terms which do not accord with his actual historical patterns of thought and language (and, therefore, has only the most indirect effect on these, if any at all). The Church may then come to be identified for all practical purposes with the hierarchy, since this closed group does and says all that it is really important to say and do; as such, instead of being mediator of faith it can become mediator of *the faith*, a very different thing, for now it mediates or hands down something to the people, presumably from God—though God never formulates the content of the faith: only men do—and so seems at least to stand between the people and God. The profession 'I believe in one, holy, Catholic and apostolic Church' can then undergo an ominous change of meaning from that given it at the opening of this paper. It can come to mean: I believe, trust, rely on the Church, for all practical purposes the official Church, rather than directly on God. And this Church in which I believe can be so a-historical that it has no effect on either the structures or the ideologies of contemporary society, apart from its attempt to read off rules for this society from some supposedly immutable law which it doesn't even claim to monopolize.

Worse may happen, as that mention of some supposedly immutable (natural) law suggests. Suppose modern man is told that in discussion of a moral topic he must not introduce any new criterion in his search for a solution (shades of *Humanae*

Vitae); that a lw of nature exists from eternity in the Logos as exemplary pattern for all that exists, and that this, like the Logos itself, is immutable. Modern man is then asked to accept a concept of divinity which may be as foreign to his experience of the world (and it is from man's experience of the world that all basic concepts of divinity come), and so may to him be as idolatrous, as the tribal god of their early ancestors, the one god amongst many, would have been to a Jew of the time of Jesus. Modern man has begun to grope again for ways of talking about God. The old Logos concept of deity from the days of Greek philosophy no longer describes the ground of being as man now understands being with its built-in mutability principle. Man is now talking, for instance, of a God who beckons from the future rather than of one who created all things according to a changeless blue-print at the beginning. His attempts to speak of God are hesitant and tentative in the extreme, as all god-talk should be; but to try to deal with him in terms of a Greek Logos-deity is again to hinder rather than help his basic instinct for faith. In such a God he can no longer believe. Such a God is as dead as the little tribal God of the wandering shepherds of ancient Israel.

Worse still can happen. Suppose that in the case of the liturgical rites in which modern man is asked to participate no adequate attempt is made to explain them to him, or the attempts to explain them which are made are couched in ideas or terms that no longer correspond to current thought or language patterns. Suppose that great lumps of a literature that ranges from 3,000 to 2,000 years old, literature from a time and culture long alien to him, the Bible I mean, suppose lumps of this are continually thrown at him during liturgical services with no attempt to translate its peculiar literary genres and thought patterns into ones he can understand. Suppose that what is supposed to be a meal looks like anything but a meal. Suppose all this, and perhaps more, and you get a man who is acting out a role in the liturgy that he does not and cannot properly understand. If he goes from a predominantly church-going population to one not like this, we may say that he loses *the faith*. That indeed is verbally precise. He has lost what he got, *the faith*. He 'gave up' the formularies and the practices he was taught. He did not lose *faith.* He probably never had it, or if he had, it survived the loss of *the faith*, which is mainly what was mediated to him. His profession and practice of *the faith* was, for the most part, superstition bordering on magic—the attempt to manipulate God by largely meaningless rites and formulae. When he over-came his superstition, when he went to a more open society and saw tolerant men make good in a life full of opportunity for all, the fear element, which is so much endemic to superstition and magic, left him, he lost *the faith*, stopped practising and professing what he once practised and professed, and whatever real faith he had underneath all the superstitition, that alone remained, but that often does remain. In this way too the Church can cease to be mediator of faith, can direct men's reliance and trust to its own clerical personnel, its own professions and practices, rather than directly to God, can stand in the way of faith rather than evoke it. This is the final tragedy of an a-historical Church.

Especially after Bonhoeffer it became the fashion to talk about religionless Christianity or secular Christianity. Not all who mouthed such slogans in imitation of Bonhoeffer knew what that prophet of our times meant. Nor is it easy to say. He said himself, 'as usual, I am being led on more by an instinctive feeling for questions that will arise later than by any conclusions that I have already reached about them'.[6] He did talk about Christianity without the religion that he knew. What was involved in this religion? Probably present forms of Church liturgy, for he was amazed to find in prison how little he missed church-going. He said himself that it involved metaphysics, by which I think we could take him to mean the formulation of certain philosophical concepts in which the faith of his Church was then embodied.[7] He even toyed with the idea of man becoming radically religion-less,[8] not just changing the forms of practice and formulation that made up the religious expression of faith here and now. But he did also express the possibility that 'In the traditional words and acts ... there may be something quite new and revolutionary, though we cannot as yet grasp or express it';[9] and that remains our hope.

However indecisive Bonhoeffer may have been, one thing can

certainly be said about that vague but diffuse movement known as secularization—namely, that it has within itself a healthy instinct for the truth of things, but tends to stray or be driven astray. The secular, the *saecula*, the ages in which men actually live out their radically historical existence in this world, this has always been the fountain of faith. Here in the secular, in all its concreteness and historical specificity, man meets God as the ground of his being and the Lord of his history. In his own world and his own human history Jesus too met God, his Father, and lived in such total dependence on his Father that he gave a definitive form to the faith that is possible for different generations of men. Man meets God in the secular and reacts to God in and through the secular. That is the oldest religious truth and it is one towards which the secularization movement is trying to return. But the secularization movement is prevented from reaching this truth precisely to the extent that men build an a-historical world of structures and concepts, of language and rites—that is, a world of these things that no longer corresponds to the actual historical patterns of the particular age, and then they give it out that God can only be met in their constructed world. What then can the man who respects the secular do except agree, since the *experts* on God keep telling him that God is not to be found where *he* is directing man's attention; well, not really or properly to be found there, but that God is to be found rather in their constructed a-historical world? What can secular man do except abandon God-talk to those who monopolize it in a-historical patterns of thought and behaviour, and instead try to conduct himself as best he can as an atheist? Secular man an athiest? What a paradox! Secular atheistic man is like a man dying of thirst on the verge of an oasis. Faith belongs to him and Christian faith belongs to him, and when the Church truly becomes the people of God, he will enter on his proper inheritance, and he will find words and actions to express his faith again. 'There are in human life', said Bonhoeffer, 'certain truths to which men will always return sooner or later. So there is no need to hurry; we have to be able to wait. God seeks what has been driven away' (*Eccles.* 3:15.)[10] That last sentence of Bonhoeffer's is a rather rough translation of a sentence in chapter three of Ecclesiastes, the chapter which begins with the oft-quoted words:

> There is a season for everything, a time for every occupation under heaven:
>> a time for giving birth
>> a time for dying
>> a time for planting
>> a time for uprooting what has been planted.

It is a good, hopeful sentence on which to end: God seeks what has been driven away.

Faith and Reason

P. J. McGRATH

I

THE relationship between faith and reason has been picturesquely described as follows: 'Faith and reason are two sisters who live together in the same house. Faith dwells on high, reason a little lower. But faith will never kill her sister; she will not betray the hospitality accorded to her to dwell alone.'[1]

I need hardly tell you that these are not the words of a contemporary writer. Who would take the trouble nowadays to assure reason that it is safe from attack? Today it is faith that feels threatened. But what the quotation effectively brings out is the character of the relationship between faith and reason as it was traditionally understood. There is the insistence, first of all, that there is no opposition between them. Faith and reason live peacefully together in the same house. It is true that on occasion they may appear to conflict, but this is always due to a misunderstanding concerning either the findings of reason or the content of faith.

Secondly, since faith lives on high, it needs the support of reason. There are certain things which are presupposed by faith—and which must be true therefore for the content of the faith to be true—but are not part of the faith and cannot be known by faith. What we believe by faith, we believe on the authority of God. But this presupposes that there is a God, who has spoken to man and whose word is to be trusted. So faith depends on reason to establish the existence of God, the fact of revelation and the reliability of God's word. These constitute the preamble of faith—the ladder which reason supplies to enable us to reach faith.

The third point is that while we need this ladder to ascend to the level of faith, we do not need it in order to remain there. We rely on reason to establish that there is a God who has spoken to man, but we then believe on the authority of God, not the authority of reason. The believer throws away the ladder, so to speak, once he has climbed it. The certainty of faith is not measured, therefore, by the certainty of the rational arguments which support it.

This, more or less, is how we were taught to understand the relationship between faith and reason when we were students studying theology. I can't say that we accepted what we were taught unquestioningly. We raised problems about it and we, no doubt, were often dissatisfied with the answers given to them. But, looking back, I feel now that the questions we asked were the wrong ones. What concerned us was the ability of reason to do what faith required of it. We wondered if it were possible to prove God's existence. We knew that all sorts of difficulties could be urged against the traditional arguments and we were uneasily aware that modern philosophers were reluctant to believe that reason could tell us anything about God. We wondered, too, if the fact of revelation could be satisfactorily established. Had Hume's arguments against miracles ever been answered? The problems that concerned us were, in other words, philosophical ones—important problems and ones that should be raised by any student of theology. But in our concern with them we never got round to asking the essential theological question, the one which, if asked, would have enabled us to see the other problems in a very different light: was this the correct account of the relationship between faith and reason? Was faith as dependent on philosophical argument as we had been taught?

I call this the essential question because I believe that the answer to it is 'No'. The traditional account of the relationship between faith and reason is seriously defective. As a consequence our understanding of faith was distorted and needless difficulties were created for the believer. But before enlarging on the defects of the traditional approach it is only fair to add that there is also something to be said for it. It is clear for one thing. You may not agree with it, but unlike some modern treatments of the subject, you are never at a loss to know what you are disagreeing with. A more important virtue is its insistence that faith is reasonable. It almost certainly goes too far in this respect, for it makes faith too dependent on rational argument. But one must admire the insistence that faith is not an irrational leap and that one does not have to abandon reason in order to believe. Finally, I think it is correct in holding that there is a preamble of faith not in the sense of preliminaries to faith, as the word 'preamble' suggests, but in the sense of things presupposed by faith and which must be true, therefore, for the content of the faith to be true, but are yet outside the scope of faith. But this is not to say that the content of the preamble is as the traditional theory understood it to be.

What is wrong then with the traditional theory, if there is so much to be said in its favour? It seems to me that there is a whole series of objections to be urged against it, but I will confine myself to what I regard as its most serious defects. The first objection may not seem very theological in character, but I believe it to be the most important of all. It is that the traditional account seems a long way removed from the faith of the ordinary believer. The majority of Christians know nothing about the preamble of faith. One might argue, of course, that the traditional theory takes account of this fact, for it does not say that the believer must be able to demonstrate the different elements of the preamble of faith for his faith to be reasonable, but only that human reason must have the capacity to do this. But this doesn't seem to make the case for the traditional theory any better. A belief is not reasonable merely because reasons exist for thinking it to be true. If I had believed before the Derby that Nijinsky was certain to win on the grounds that I had picked him out with a pin, my belief would have been wholly irrational even though very good reasons existed at the time for the belief that this horse would indeed win. The reasonableness of a belief clearly requires that the believer be aware of some good reason in its favour. Hence the faith of the average Christian cannot be made reasonable by arguments or reasons which he knows nothing about.

One might continue to defind the traditional position by saying —'So much the worse then for the average believer. This only goes to show that his faith is imperfect.' But again this seems to me to be unrealistic. The function of the theologian is to explain the faith as he finds it, not as he would wish it to be. In any event, if we want a model of the Christian faith, we should look not to the theologians, but to the saints. How many of the apostles, for instance, knew anything of the proofs for God's existence or for the divine veracity? No doubt if put to it, they would have been able to formulate an argument to show that Christ was a divine emissary. But what seems certain is that this had little to do with their own belief in Christ as the Son of God. So it seems that the traditional theory explains the reasonableness of faith only at the expense of making the faith of the majority unreasonable. And this is sufficient to condemn it.

A second objection could be stated as follows: the traditional theory insisted that for faith to be reasonable, man must be capable of knowing that God exists by reason alone. This compelled the believer to consider the question of God's existence in isolation from revelation. So when Catholics asked themselves: does God really exist or is he merely a product of man's mind?, they inevitably assumed that the question could be answered only in terms of philosophical argument. This assumption was, I believe, both wrong and dangerous. Wrong, because if God has really spoken to man as we believe, then that is surely the best possible witness to his existence: what better evidence could you have for the existence of God than that he has revealed himself to man? And dangerous, because anyone who confines himself to the philosophical arguments for God's existence is not to be blamed too seriously if he ends up in atheism. If one considers the universe, its existence and the wonderful order which is present everywhere in it, it is easy to believe in a creator. But as soon as one tries to formulate an argument to show that there must be a creator to account for the existence or order of the universe, the whole thing seems to dissolve in doubts and ambiguities. I do not wish to suggest that the arguments for God's existence are devoid of all validity. But anyone who has spent some time studying them, is unlikely to regard them as very useful instruments for producing certainty about the existence of God.

But if you use revelation as a testimony to the existence of God, aren't you in danger of arguing in a circle? How could one know that a revelation had occurred without first knowing that there was a God who was capable of revealing himself? This is obviously a crucial question and I will try to deal with it more fully later on. All I wish to say for the moment is this: every argument for God's existence is based on a real or supposed revelation of God. For if the Christian God exists, the entire universe is a revelation of God to man, though not a revelation in precisely the same sense as the Bible. So in arguing to God, what one is endeavouring to do is to show that the universe or some aspect of it is genuinely revelatory. If it were true, therefore, that one could not identify a revelation as genuine without first knowing that God exists, one could never provide any reason for believing in God, for to try to do so would be to involve oneself in an infinite regress.

A third difficulty with the traditional approach is that the account which it gives of the relationship between reason and faith seems to make no sense. What it says is that the believer needs the help provided by reason to reach the level of faith, but once that level is reached, reason may be dispensed with. The believer then abstracts from the rational arguments that support faith and rests his faith entirely on the authority of God.

One cannot help feeling that the traditional approach is here trying to have it both ways. For it is claiming that faith is reasonable and so requires the support of reason, but that any difficulties arising in the rational arguments that support faith do not take from its certainty. But how can faith be both dependent on and independent of reason at the same time? The answer to this difficulty is always given in the form of an image—that of an individual using a ladder to reach a new level and then throwing away the ladder once he has got there. But does this image fit the situation? Can the preamble of faith be dispensed with by the believer, given the role which the traditional theory assigns to it? To answer this question we must ask another: what is the precise character of the relationship between the premable of faith and the content of faith? There are only two possible answers. The relation can be either logical or psychological. It is psychological if you need the preamble of faith in order to believe, but the truth of the faith is then independent of the truth of the preamble —just as Doubting Thomas needed to see the risen Christ to believe in the resurrection, but the truth of the resurrection is not in any way dependent on Thomas having seen the risen Lord. It is logical if the truth of faith is logically dependent on the truth of the preamble. An example would be the relationship between the truth of the resurrection and the truth of the proposition 'The dead body of Christ is no longer in the tomb.'

Now the relation between the preamble of faith and the content of faith cannot be merely psychological. We don't need a knowledge of the preamble in order to believe since a good many believers know nothing of it. The relation must therefore be logical in character. But this means that the truth of the faith is logically dependent on the truth of the preamble and anything which tends to undermine the validity of the preamble will tend to undermine the faith itself. The believer cannot, in other words, dispense with the preamble as soon as he reaches the level of faith, for if the traditional theory is correct, his faith remains always dependent on reason for support. The image which fits the situation, then, is not that of a climber throwing away the ladder once he has reached a new level, but that of someone, sawing off the branch on which he is sitting.

We are now in a position to see the fundamental ambiguity in the traditional theory. When it insists on the necessity of the preamble for faith to be reasonable it is treating the relation between the two as logical. But when it claims that the believer can dispense with the preamble, it is treating it as merely psychological. And there is no way of resolving this inconsistency. For if the traditional theory were to plump unreservedly for the logical character of the relationship, it would be destroying faith, or at least seriously distorting it, since the certainty of faith would then derive from reason rather than from God. Whereas if it were to decide that the relationship were not logical after all, it would be destroying itself, since the preamble would not then be necessary for faith in any sense.

II

One could extend this list of objections, but perhaps it would be more useful if at this stage we adopted a different approach. Let us instead try to get some little way inside the mind of the people who put forward the traditional theory. How did a theory with so many defects exercise such a strong hold on Catholic thought for so long. As students why did it never occur to us to question its validity? The answer, I believe, is simple enough. The traditional account of the relationship between faith and reason was a consequence—I should say almost a necessary consequence —of the traditional understanding of revelation. Faith is man's response to divine revelation. Now revelation was traditionally understood as the communication of propositions and the result of revelation was a body of truth which had been communicated by God to man. Faith was therefore the acceptance of these truths by the individual. But how was the individual believer to know that these propositions were worthy of acceptance? The only possible answer is that he would have to show by rational argument that there is a God who has revealed these things to man. Once you accept the propositional view of revelation you are committed to the traditional theory of the relation between reason and faith. The only alternative is to say that faith is irrational, that it is simply the blind acceptance of certain propositions for which no justification can be provided.

As we all know this propositional view of revelation is now outmoded. The Second Vatican Council has taught us that revelation is God revealing and communicating himself to man, not communicating propositions merely. The primary purpose of revelation is to allow us to enter into a fellowship, a personal communion, with God, rather than to increase our store of information. This restoration by the Vatican Council of the biblical concept of revelation has enormous implications for theology and for the Christian life and it may be some time before we have fully appreciated all of them. But one implication seems obvious enough—it demands a rethinking of the nature of faith and particularly of the relationship between faith and reason. For if faith is our response to God's revelation of himself, it makes no sense to say that we need to be able to prove God's existence for our faith to be reasonable. Why should we need to have God as the conclusion of an argument if by faith we are already in contact with him as a person? You don't need to prove the existence of someone you already know.

There is a well-known distinction in philosophy between knowledge by acquaintance and knowledge by description.[2] You have knowledge by acquaintance of someone if you are personally acquainted with him; you have knowledge by description alone if, though not personally acquainted, you are in possession of certain facts about him. Of course, knowledge by acquaintance includes knowledge by description, since one could not be personally acquainted with someone without knowing certain facts about him. The point I wish to make, however, is this: the most that philosophical argument can provide about God is knowledge by description. And this sort of knowledge is insufficient for faith if faith is directed towards the person of God rather than towards a set of propositions. And not merely is it insufficient, it is unnecessary since it is included in the knowledge of God given to us by faith. In other words, if faith really brings us into personal contact with God, we don't need the knowledge of God which is to be gained from rational argument. But if faith does not do this, then rational argument cannot make good that defect.

This distinction between knowledge by acquaintance and knowledge by description goes some distance towards ending the dispute between Catholic theologians and the followers of Karl Barth on our knowledge of God. When Barth says that 'God is always the One who has made himself known to man in his revelation, and not the one man thinks out for himself and describes as God',[3] what he says is perfectly acceptable if we understand him as referring to knowledge of God by acquaintance. And indeed that is what Barth must be referring to since he is concerned with the knowledge that saves, the knowledge of God that is essential to faith. When Barth's opponents, on the other hand, assert that there is also a natural knowledge of God apart from revelation, then again what they are asserting is true provided one understands it as referring only to knowledge of God by description. I am not suggesting, of course, that this distinction removes all the differences between Barthian and Catholic theologians on the question of our knowledge of God. But neglect of the distinction by both parties to the dispute has needlessly exaggerated the difference between them.

There is no question then of proving God's existence as a preliminary to faith. A proof is superfluous if faith does what it claims and puts us in personal contact with God, and it is inadequate if faith doesn't do this. Still less is it necessary to prove God's truthfulness. The demand for such a proof is in fact quite incompatible with faith. It is equivalent to saying 'I will not accept the reliability of God's word unless it can be proved to me that what he says is true.' To realize how far removed this is from the attitude of mutual trust that is demanded by faith, one has only to visualize a husband or wife saying it about their partner. The demand for proof of reliability is an expression, not of trust, but of the lack of it. And even if a satisfactory proof is forthcoming, all that has been established is the sort of relationship that exists between a bank and a client who has provided security for a loan—a relationship of trust, if you wish, but based not on personal trust, but on the realities of business. There is no need to emphasize how unlike this is to the response God expects of his people.

This brings us to the third item in the traditional preamble of faith—the fact of revelation. Is it necessary to establish the historical fact of revelation for our faith to be reasonable? This is a difficult and complex question and it would be easy to over-simplify it. A basic preliminary consideration is this: Christianity is a religion that is both historical and trans-historical in character. It is historical because it is centred on Christ, a man who lived at a particular time and place; and it is trans-historical because the Christ we believe in is not simply the man who once lived on earth, but the risen Christ who transcends space and time and who is present here and now in the Church. The historical character of Christianity, which is in many respects a guarantee of the validity of Christian beliefs, has now become a serious obstacle to faith for many people. It isn't merely the problem of establishing the historical facts—though that is problem enough— but that in an era of constant change like the present it is difficult to accept that what happened even fifty years ago has any relevance to the present age, never mind what happened at a distance of two thousand years. The Church has helped to accentuate this difficulty by clinging to the outward forms of the past. Until very recently, when one thought of the Church, the image that came to mind was that of a medieval building in which a man clad in garments from ancient Rome worshipped in a language that has not been used colloquially for nearly two thousand years. We can hardly be surprised if people sometimes treat Christianity as belonging more properly to the museum than to the market place.

There has been a tendency in recent times, particularly in modern Protestant theology, to respond to this problem by minimizing the historical character of Christianity, by saying 'What happened historically is unimportant, all that matters is our present faith.' But what happened historically clearly cannot be unimportant for Christianity, since the Incarnation is an event which occurred at a particular time and place or it is nothing. The proper response to the difficulty is not to minimize either the historical or the trans-historical character of Christianity, but to give full value to both. Now while at present the tendency may be to minimize the historical character of Christianity, in the past the reverse was the case. The traditional presentation of faith, by overemphasizing the historical aspect of Christianity, neglected its trans-historical character. The revelation to which our faith was a response was, according to that presentation, the revelation that took place in biblical times. But if revelation ended two thousand years ago we are back with the propositional view of revelation. What has been revealed to us is not God himself, but certain truths about the revelation of himself to others. For God to reveal himself to us, revelation must be a present reality and it is to this present revelation that our faith is directed.

We don't need to prove the fact of revelation as a preliminary to faith, therefore, since in faith we are confronted with the fact of revelation and our faith is a response to it. For us the fact of revelation is Christ, but not someone seen dimly at a distance of two thousand years, whose life and teachings are laboriously reconstructed by biblical scholars and historians, but the Christ who is present here and now in the Church. Through faith we become contemporaries of Christ. For believers he is a figure from our own time rather than from the past. In Christ are summed up the three elements in the traditional preamble of faith—the existence of God, the truthfulness of God's word and the fact of revelation. Christ is God revealing himself to man— 'To have seen me is to have seen the Father' (*John* 14:9). He is God's Word, and we accept the truthfulness of that Word not by satisfying ourselves of the validity of a philosophical argument but by personal adherence to Christ in faith. And finally, as I have just said, he is the revelation to which our faith is a response. Once we realize that our faith is directed to the person of Christ rather than to a set of propositions the superfluous character of the traditional preamble of faith becomes immediately apparent. To put it bluntly, it is a mental construction of doubtful validity designed to fulfil a non-existent need.

To say that our faith is a response to a present revelaton is not, however, to imply that what happened in history is irrelevant to faith. The truth of Christianity depends on certain historical claims and Christianity would be refuted, therefore, if these claims were shown to be false. As believing Christians we cannot be indifferent to historical research. But this is not to say that our faith is based on the findings of historians. St Paul said to his disciples in Corinth: 'If Christ has not been raised, then our preaching is useless, and your believing it is useless' (1 *Cor.* 15:14). But he himself believed in the resurrection not primarily because he had satisfied himself of its genuine historical character, but because he had met the risen Christ on the road to Damascus. So as Christians we believe in the resurrection because through faith we meet Christ in today's world. We accept the empty tomb because we believe that the risen Christ is present here and now in the Church. This admittedly is not the only reason we accept it. If historical research can undermine the faith, then it follows that it can also corroborate it. And the testimony of history is no doubt an important corroboration of faith, but it is not the basis of it. The certainty of faith cannot be derived from the uncertainties of history.

III

There is still one important question to be asked about faith and reason and I will devote the rest of this paper to an attempt to answer it. The conception of faith that I have outlined leaves faith self-sufficient so to speak. True, it is still linked to both reason and history, in that reason or history could show it to be false, but it does not absolutely require the positive support of either of them. But how then can we know that our faith has objective validity? If faith is a response to present revelation, have we any assurance that revelation is a reality, that it isn't simply an illusion on our part? How do we recognize this revelation? Is it a special experience which only believers possess?

In an area where there are many uncertainties one thing can be stated with a fair degree of assurance: faith is not based on a special experience. This is not to say, of course, that faith may not involve special experiences, and there can be no doubt that such experiences do occur in the lives of believers, bringing home to them the reality of God in a new and more telling way. But these cannot be the basis of faith. Of their nature they are exceptional in character and fleeting in nature, whereas faith must be based on something which is constant and is common to all believers.

Perhaps the best way to answer our question is by turning back once more to the apostles. What distinguished them from the onlookers who refused to believe? Not any special experience. Some of them did indeed have a special experience on Mount Tabor, but this was not the basis of their faith. Generally speaking the apostles and disciples had precisely the same experiences as those who saw Christ and did not believe. What distinguished them was their way of experiencing, their way of looking at what they saw. For while unbelievers looked at Jesus and saw only a man who gave forth human doctrines, his disciples looked at him and saw the Christ, the Son of the living God, whose words were the words of eternal life. To have faith, therefore, is to see things from a special and unique point of view. St Thomas says somewhere that in faith we see with the eye of God. To have faith is to see things as God sees them, but in a very imperfect way, of course: 'Now we are seeing a dim reflection in a mirror' (1 *Cor.* 13:12). The believer sees the universe not as unexplainable matter, but as a revelation of God, as a sacrament of God's presence. He sees the Bible not as an interesting historical document, but as the word of God. He sees the liturgy as making Christ present to the community of believers. He sees other people as making demands on him in the name of Christ. And he sees all these things as the revelation of God to man in the person of Jesus.

But having said all that, the same nagging question recurs: has this way of looking at things objective validity or is it merely a delusion? Is it reasonable to look on reality with the eye of faith? Our natural instinct when confronted with this question is to try to provide a justification of faith from outside of faith. This instinct has been reinforced by our theological training, for that is precisely the task which traditional apologetics set itself—to justify faith without presupposing faith. And the traditional preamble of faith was the result of its efforts.

Now I believe this instinct to be false and this effort to be mis-directed. For, in the first place, it doesn't succeed. Of course, it doesn't completely fail either. You *can* make a case for the validity of faith without presupposing faith. But the response of an objective and uncommitted observer to this would be, 'Perhaps', or, 'Not improbable'—not the response that faith requires, which is, 'I believe, Lord, help my unbelief.'

However, the principal objection to traditional apologetics is not that it fails to make good its claim to establish the validity of faith, but that it argues with unbelief on the unbeliever's own terms. What the unbeliever says is that if Christianity is true, then it must be possible to state the case for Christianity in a way that is equally accessible to both the believer and the unbeliever. Traditional apologetics accepted this and the argument is put forward was consequently regarded as *the* case for Christianity. The validity of faith was held to stand or fall by the validity of the case made in apologetics.

This, I think, is quite wrong and in fact is seriously harmful to faith. For the certainty of faith derives not from outside faith, but from faith itself. You cannot appreciate the case for the validity of faith unless you are already a believer. In saying this

I am not myself presupposing the validity of faith. I am not saying that faith is such that the believer must be mistaken. What I am saying is that faith is such that the unbeliever cannot appreciate fully the case for Christianity. You cannot appreciate the reasons for accepting Christ as the Son of God unless you expose yourself to God's revelation of himself in Christ, and this means accepting the Christian faith.

But doesn't this mean that faith is circular, that you cannot appreciate the truth of the premises of the argument for faith unless you have first accepted the conclusion? The answer, I think, is 'Yes'. There is a circularity involved in faith in that what we regard as evidence for the validity of faith would not appear as evidence at all, or would appear as evidence only in a very dubious sense, unless we were already believers. We agree with the Psalmist that the heavens declare the glory of God and the firmament proclaims his handiwork, but we do so only because we already believe in God; if we didn't believe in God, the heavens would declare nothing but their own glory. Or take Newman's description of the phenomenon of conscience: 'If we feel responsibility, are ashamed, are frightened, it is because there is One to whom we are responsible, before whom we are ashamed, whose claims upon us we fear.'[4] If we didn't already believe in the existence of a God who is guardian of the moral order, we would look upon this interpretation of conscience as a delusion. Or take mircles. What better evidence could you have, one might say, for the validity of faith than the miracles which Christ performed or which have since occurred in the Church? But the trouble is that unless one already accepts faith in at least a minimal sense, these events won't appear as miracles. The unbeliever will either take the view that because of their inherently improbable character, it is highly unlikely that they ever occurred, or else the view that we don't yet know how to explain these events scientifically, but eventually we will be able to do so. We are inclined to say that the unbeliever is being unreasonable, that he is failing to face up to the facts. But he is being unreasonable only on our terms, not on his own.

A miracle provides evidence for the validity of faith only if you interpret it religiously; and to describe it as a miracle is already to see it from the religious point of view.

Does this circularity mean that faith is irrational? If we are using the normally accepted idea of rationality, then the answer is 'Yes'. Western thought has taken its concept of rationality from Descartes, the father of rationalism, who explained rationality and defined rationalism in one sentence of his work, *A Discourse on Method*, where he laid it down as a rule for himself 'to hold nothing as true that cannot be clearly proved to me'. This innocent-looking rule has taken such a hold on men's minds that nowadays one could say almost that people are born as rationalists; it is part of the air we breathe. What we are inclined to forget is the history of rationalism. We overlook the fact that only a hundred years separate Descartes' *Discourse on Method* from Hume's *Treatise of Human Nature*. It took only a hundred years for Descartes' optimism about human reason to be transformed into the melancholy which Hume expresses at the end of Book I of his *Treatise* when he decides that nothing is certain.

During those hundred years men discovered that had Descartes applied his concept or rationality more consistently, then not merely would he have begun his philosophy with a universal doubt, but he would have ended it in the same way. For his idea of rationality is impossibly narrow. It is taken from mathematics and in mathematics it is, of course, true to say that you don't know something unless you can prove it. But mathematics bears little relation to other branches of knowledge. As Hume showed in his *Treatise*, Descartes' concept of rationality produces scepticism not merely about religious faith, but about knowledge in general. For the circularity which we have discovered in faith is typical of every aspect of knowledge. Take sense knowledge; philosophers have devoted an enormous amount of energy to endeavouring to prove its objectivity, to showing that there is an external world which possesses the features that our senses reveal to us. And their effort has ended in almost total failure, a failure much more complete than the failure of apologetics to provide an external justification for Christianity. Now there is in fact no difficulty in presenting a case for the validity of sense knowledge. What could be better evidence for its validity than the fact that what our senses have presented us with hitherto has always, or almost always, been really there. But this, of course, presupposes the validity of our senses, for how could we know that what we saw was really there unless we already regarded our senses as reliable? And this circularity is only to be expected, since the certainty of sense perception derives from sense perception itself; it cannot be derived from outside. Or take scientific knowledge: it is now widely accepted that, despite its air of utter rationality, there is no way of providing a rational justification of scientific procedure. In every scientific argument there is an unstated premise on whose truth the validity of the argument depends—that the laws of nature which held good in the past will also hold good in the future. But there is no way of establishing the truth of this premise either within science or outside it. You can only take it on trust. But in another sense there is no difficulty in providing a justification for science. For what could be better evidence for its validity than the tremendous success of science in the past. However, this too involves us in circularity. The past success of science is evidence of its future success only if we assume that the future will be like the past; and this is to assume the validity of the scientific outlook, the very point at issue. Again this circularity is there because the certainty of science derives from science itself, not from outside. Or take ethics: is there any way of justifying ethics, of establishing that moral judgements are objective and not expressions merely of subjective likes and dislikes? The familiar answer is that this can be done only within ethics in the circular fashion I have outlined. If you try to provide an external justification, you inevitably get involved in the fallacy of deriving 'ought' from 'is'. For the certainty attaching to moral judgements derives from ethics itself and not from outside.

This circularity which we find in every branch of human knowledge is not just an unexpected fact; it is something that couldn't be otherwise. For to prove something is always to leave something else unproven, and our arguments, no matter how far back we push them, always presuppose something that we accept without argument, something whose certainty derives from itself and not from outside. Furthermore, if sense perception or science or ethics are unique and irreducible ways of looking at reality, it is only to be expected that they cannot be justified from outside; such a justification would imply that they were not unique after all, but were reducible to some more fundamental way of seeing reality. It is not surprising then if we find the same circularity in faith, since the eye of faith is certainly unique and irreducible to any other form of knowledge. This circularity is a token of its reationality rather than the reverse.

Well, is faith reasonable then? It is reasonable in the sense of not offending against the negative criteria of rationality, provided we take these criteria from human knowledge as it actually exists and not from some *a priori* model as Descartes did. But there is another more positive sense of rationality in which to say that faith is reasonable is to say that the evidence in its favour warrants the certainty that the believer feels about its validity. Is faith reasonable in that sense? This question I cannot answer for you, since it is a question each person has to answer for himself. Your answer to that question is what constitutes your faith or lack of it, and the decision to believe, like all the great decisions of life, is one that the individual, in the last analysis, must make alone.

The Way of Faith

WILLIAM J. PHILBIN

St Augustine's saying that the processes of nature are much more worthy of wonder than the occasional miracle which upsets them is a useful warning against ignoring the commonplace Miracles, he assumes, being unusual, cannot fail to make an impact. The whole content of Christianity, which includes matter communicated by God to all men through the endowment of reason as well as things conveyed by direct revelation, may be thought of as typified in St Augustine's distinction. And we may go on to see in what he says a hint that in the broad field of belief and behaviour it is the ordinary and shared truths of religion that need emphasis, information that comes in an extraordinary way being in no danger of neglect. To the extent that most of our day-to-day moral difficulties are concerned with principles that are largely common ground with others, such a line of thought has validity. But it would be dangerous to assume that what exceeds the order of nature in our religion may not become obscured or put out of sight.

Time and custom diminish the impression made by any kind of experience: having lived in a landscape or a city all one's life often means that even its outstanding features have never been properly appreciated. As Christianity comes within a generation of completing its second millennium it is showing some distressing symptoms of this kind of failure in self-knowledge. All loss is serious in proportion to the value of what is forfeited. In our case this could hardly be overrated. Revelation has introduced into our religious thinking certain features which dominate the whole scene.

Even more significant than the extent of what is new is the

fact that we are asked to accept it as new, as coming directly from God and therefore to be believed on his word as beyond our questioning or modification. The content of what we receive, remarkable as it is, is not so much in need of emphasis as this character and quality of God-given which colours every part of it. This establishes for believers a unique association with God. To realize clearly this foremost truth about our religion is to make the correct approach to its understanding and at the same time to provide a corrective for currents of opinion which are tending to set Christianity adrift from its moorings.

I

Unless we realize what individuates our religion we cannot be said really to know it at all. Christianity is different because it has proclaimed itself from the beginning a unique visitation and communication from God. If it is not this it is simply a deception and we are 'most miserable of all men' (1 *Cor*. 15:19). That it represents man's best religious thinking and highest ideals is not a tenable second line of defence: its essential position will have been penetrated if the credentials it offers are rejected. In the course of history innumerable claims have been made of direct interventions of divinity in different fashions and with varying degrees of response from mankind. But no other system—not even Judaism in which it began—has been so committed to certain detailed historical records of supramundane origins and so centred on acceptance of one human being as divine and as sole source of salvation, putting more emphasis on the drama and *dramatis personae* of its beginning than on the plausibility of its doctrines. No other has spelt out so uncompromisingly a system of belief so extensive and explicit, and none has had so vast an impact on human living.

That Christian principles should be widely admired and followed on their inherent merits is obviously welcome: it is agreeable to have the term 'Christian' used as a synonym for what is good-natured and unselfish. But Christianity must not become a common noun. Its typical expression is to be love of others, but belief in its claimed origins and acceptance of its

special assistance towards the exercise of love are the irreducible
terms on which it is offered. It comes by way of gift and we are
asked to acknowledge the gift as gift, not to imagine it is of human
devising or ours by natural right, so that we may mould it in
each generation into whatever form we will.

St John places Christianity in full setting and perspective in
the prologue to his gospel. Its background, extending through
eternity, is the co-existence with God and in God of a second
Person who in the first instance was the agent of creation, the life
and the light of all men (*John* 1:14). In Christ he has come among
men in visible form 'full of grace and truth', a description that is
emphasized by repetition (*John* 1:14 and 17), inviting men to
something more than their ordinary relationship with God,
giving them power 'to become children of God' (*John* 1:12).
The new status is thrust on no one, indeed rejection figures more
prominently than acceptance, the exercise of free choice being
crucial. Adherence to Christ involves enormously enriching
consequences. Those who 'receive him', who 'believe in him',
receive 'from his fullness' 'grace upon grace' (*John* 1:16), 'grace
and truth' (*John* 1:17). The transfiguration can only be described
as rebirth into a new life—a description St John's gospel uses in
all more than fifty times. Being children of God means (if we
follow the more generally accepted text) being born again, and
this time 'not of the will of blood nor of the flesh nor of the will
of man, but of God' (*John* 1:13).

In a little space St John maps out here the main features of
the Christian dispensation. It is not, as is being so often suggested
nowadays, a matter of a highly gifted human being gradually
coming to realize a divine vocation and delivering his message
according to the growth of his knowledge. It is an account of the
Son of the Father as found in Colossians (1:15 ff.) and in
Hebrews (1:1 ff.), one who pre-existed all creation and in whom
'the fullness of God was pleased to dwell', coming to offer
privileges not implicit in the responsibilities, if one may use the
word, assumed by God in bringing man into existence. It is not
a stage in man's long endeavour to know and come to terms with
divinity, it is not even the peak of achievement in these efforts.
It is not comparable with upsurges of energy or genius of which

history records many instances. It is entirely a divine initiative, transacted once for all 'when the fullness of time was come' (*Gal.* 4:4) by someone who was God as well as man. 'God was in Christ reconciling the world to himself' (2 *Cor.* 5:19).

This for St John and St Paul is what is first and most fundamental about our religion: it is not ours in its making, nor is it innate; it is a gift, though a gift we have to make an effort to apprehend. If we are to speak exactly there are no born Catholics. By corollary, we need to exert ourselves in order to retain this gift—like other powers it is to be maintained by the same arts that gained it. It is not for nothing that the Church prescribes among necessary acts of religion formal expressions of belief in doctrine on the grounds of God's word. That it is conferred only on certain conditions does not detract from its overall character of gift. Indeed the chief condition required, the test of faith, implies a conferring of knowledge as well as the demand of credence. Faith, with overtones of trust, self-surrender and many other religious dispositions, means basically the intellectual acceptance following a decision of the will, of something not discerned by oneself.

To minimize the element of sacrifice, of self-denial, inherent in this relationship would be misleading. Faith in the New Testament is a unique kind of disposition, going far beyond the fidelity and trust demanded by God of his chosen people under the Old Covenant. In our Lord's teaching it began with acceptance of his authority: there is no evading the fact that this is his primary demand. From this it gradually enlarges itself into belief in many specific assertions and promises. With the apostles, as witness especially St Paul, the redemptive death and resurrection of Christ are ceaselessly dwelt on, and other aspects of doctrine and directives concerning Christian living become prominent. As revelation is more fully eludicated by the Church authority which Christ had set up, the range of what is required continually widens.

Other aspects of faith go further to signalize its distinctiveness. If charity is to be the virtue marking out Christians in their living, faith is the attitude that constitutes them Christians: they they are called simply 'those who believe' (*Mark* 16:16; *John*

7:39). So representative is this assent and submission that it can be the name of the whole religious response, everything else that is required being taken as an obvious consequence of this initial step. 'The just man lives by faith' (*Rom*. 1:17). It is a surrender to divine guidance of a most decisive and absolute kind, making God's word the overriding rule of thinking and living, so that liberty of opinion is given up in the areas covered by his word and its authoritative interpretation. The new 'way'—a description that recurs throughout the New Testament—is the acceptance of guidance.

The absoluteness of what St Paul calls 'the obedience of faith' (*Rom*. 1:5; 16:26) is its outstanding feature. Notable about its content is the fact that it does not deal merely with points of doctrine or morals where men had got some way already: we are not only offered assurance about truths we partly knew previously or given a clear lead on doubtful issues, although such help is provided. The body of doctrine that Christianity asks to be believed is characterized by a number of large assertions which entirely exceed the range of our understanding and experience and which can be accepted only on the word of God, only by virtue of our unquestioning confidence in his all-knowledge and truthfulness. Not only that, even when we can find a formula of words that conveys some information about these realities, we find ourselves regularly unable to conceive how they can be realized, how their several facets can co-exist. We deceive ourselves if we try to disguise the fact that faith is a challenge. One article of our creed after another makes it plain that the essence of the test is deference on the part of our intelligence to God's transcendent knowledge.

It is typical that the resurrection of our Lord was placed in the forefront of the Pentecostal preaching of the apostles and that St Paul included the resurrection of the body in his address to the Athenians. Other incongruities were to follow. That there should be three Persons really distinct from one another in a single divine being is something we are required unhesitatingly to affirm, although ultimately the only help our philosophizing can offer is the observation that the Infinite must be expected to enfold reality of a kind our short-range understanding cannot penetrate. Trinitarian doctrine is our safeguard against anthropomorphism. A whole complex of mysteries is presented in the Incarnation, involving not only the living of the Son of God in a man of our flesh and blood but such a union as leaves in Christ only a single Person. And we must believe too that this divine Person, by his humiliation and death as man, saved us and gained us the divine favour, setting the seal on our redemption in the culmination of his miracles, the Resurrection. What is taught about the next life, with its dreadful contrast of alternatives, is another area that presents difficulties to our judgement.

Faith then in its nature, in the quality of its assent and in the outstanding features of its content is not something that fits tidily into human ways of thinking. It is not a predictable arrangement for men who can think and reason and decide for themselves. There is an inevitable tendency of human intelligence, particularly when its proneness to self-conceit is indulged, to repudiate what it cannot confirm or understand. St Paul startlingly declares that what is most significant about Christianity is folly to worldly wisdom. 'Has not God made foolish the wisdom of the world? For since in the wisdom of the world the world did not know God through wisdom, it pleased God through the folly of what we preach to save those who believe . . . For the foolishness of God is wiser than man' (1 *Cor.* 1:20-25). The same point is made by our Lord: 'I bless you, Father, Lord of Heaven and earth, for hiding these things from the learned and clever and revealing them to mere children' (*Matt.* 11:25). In the Apostolic Church there were 'not many wise according to the worldly standards' (1 *Cor.* 1:26) and in every age we must be prepared to find self-confident human reason rejecting what is beyond the range of its vision and comprehension.

Recognition of the nature of faith and of its place as the linchpin of our religion is a matter of first importance in any attempt to find a clear way through a chaos of ideas that are causing much bewilderment and distress today. We are experiencing a widespread tendency to diminish or ignore the demand faith makes upon us, in so far as it goes beyond a mere generalized acceptance of Christ—something he refers to as calling him 'Lord, Lord' (*Matt.* 7:21)—and extends to belief in a body of doctrine originating from his preaching and elucidated under his authority. We cannot remain Christian and allow human opinion to substitute for divine authority as the criterion of what should be believed. And we may not quietly set aside the element of mystery in our creed or leave unmentioned what is other-worldly and incongruous as subjects in bad taste in our sophisticated age. We must have the courage to accept the 'shame' of the cross (*Heb.* 12:2)—and the shame of the Resurrection. We cannot reduce Christianity to earthly dimensions and we must endure the penalties of being different. In his last words to his apostles, our Lord emphasized that although they are in the world and he is sending them into the world, they are not of the world, that he has taken them out of the world (*John* 17:6, 9, 14, 16, 18). Sayings like those tend to be kept out of sight today.

The apparent contradiction in these words of our Lord serves as a reminder that what is being stressed is not the whole story. In insisting on the element of the extraordinary, the ultra in our religion, one must leave place for what reason has been able to discover by itself, for the component of old and widely shared wisdom. The parables are full of homespun practical good sense that can be paralleled in folk-lore and proverb everywhere. The preacher of the Kingdom 'brings out of his treasure old things and new' (*Matt.* 13:52). It was part of the concern of our Lord and of the evangelists to insist on what was traditional in order to establish ancestry and legitimacy. Nevertheless newness is the feature that comes increasingly to be stressed as Christianity begins to know itself and stand on its feet. What comes with Christ is new wine that will not be contained in old bottles, a new cloth that will not serve as patching for old garments (*Matt.* 9:16). 'A new doctrine' is how his first hearers described what he preached (*Mark* 1:27) and the Athenians were also struck by this feature of newness (*Acts* 17:19-20). For St Paul the Christian becomes 'a new man' (*Eph.* 4:24), 'a new creation, the old has passed away' (2 *Cor.* 5:17 and *Gal.* 6:15), he 'walks in newness of life' (*Rom.* 6:4).

In foscusing on what is most significant we must guard also against any impression of standing for a mere passive receiving and preservation of a set of inert ideas. The nature of our creed

is not the less God-given for being influenced by human intelligence in the direction of change and development. If we must
guard against the lure of a secular outlook on the one hand,
there is on the other the menace of stagnation, obscurantism and
complacency to be taken account of. Too often the Church has
allowed a back-log of necessary adjustments to pile up, with
unfortunate consequences. Vatican II was expressly summoned
to deal with such a situation and to put into effect such developments as Vatican I had recognized as having always been a
factor in the Church's life. Two forces must be reconciled here:
one making for movement, the other conserving.

St Paul knows of both of these. He is often tentative and un-
decided and hortatory, allowing room for views differing from
his own personal judgements and for fuller understanding of
what had been revealed; indeed his letters reveal that his own
opinions on some matters were subject to development. But there
is no doubt about where he believes the main emphasis must rest.
'Guard the truth that has been entrusted to you by the Holy
Spirit who dwells in you' is his repeated charge to Timothy
(2 *Tim*. 1:14; 1 *Tim*. 6:20). The tendency to alter things unchangeable was encountered by him and he repeatedly inveighed against
it, sometimes in language that could hardly be more forceful.
'Even if we, or an angel from heaven', he writes to the 'foolish
Galatians', 'should preach to you a gospel at variance with that
which we have preached to you, let him be accursed' (*Gal*. 1:8-9).
The overriding concern is, as St. Jude put it, to 'contend for the
faith once delivered to the saints' (*Jude* 3). Our Lord had promised
the Spirit whose gift of knowledge and understanding is described
as elucidating what he had taught, though often to the uncom-
prehending (*John* 14:26; 16:14).

Development is part of the Church's duty but it is development
in fidelity to the original deposit of faith. It must always check
with the past. The system of dual control was set out already in
the fifth century by St Vincent of Lerins: 'But some of you will
say perhaps: Is there then to be no progress in Christ Church?
Progress certainly and that the greatest . . . But progress, mind
you, of such sort that it is a true advance, and not a change in
the faith. For progress implies a growth within the thing itself,

while change turns one thing into another. Consequently, the understanding, knowledge and wisdom of each and all—of each churchman and of the whole Church—ought to grow and progress greatly and eagerly through the course of ages and centuries, provided that the advance be within its own lines, in the same sphere of doctrine, the same feeling, the same sentiment.'[1]

The principle of development is being invoked nowadays in support of many alterations at variance with the deposit of faith and deviating from interpretations of that deposit to which the Church has committed herself. One sometimes feels that Christianity is being thought of as a school of opinion or a social theory so susceptible of modifications that it may in the course of time take away or reverse any of its original features, that it is the first stage in a train of thinking to be improved on indefinitely without regard to its original content—a concept as endlessly variable as 'democracy'. If, as is suggested by phrases like 'what modern man will accept', 'the feeling of the present generation', 'the new Christianity that is being born out of the old', the source of what we believe is to become not revelation but fashions of human opinion, we are indeed encountering a change which 'turns one thing into another' and which in fact alters the central basis and criterion of all belief by changing the ultimate ground on which all doctrines are believed.

One evidence of this shift of position is the increasing neglect of the Bible in much that is being written about theological subjects. In an age which was hailed as marking a return to the Scriptures many writings are appearing which are satisfied with a mere courtesy reference to a few texts from the inspired books. Theology nowadays is all too often regarded as under no obligation to consider how its speculation compares with the biblical evidence. Still less is any duty recognized to examine the teaching of a Church magisterium whose function in regard to doctrine is so clearly laid down in Scripture.

Another indication of the tendency to regard doctrine merely as a human property is found in a way of thinking about theology as an academic discipline to be treated like any secular field of study. 'Theology' may connote a wide complex of mundane studies and clearly, where matters such as comparative religion and linguistic or historical research are concerned, its methods and responsibilities are those of any other branch of scholarship. 'Theology' in the sense of religious belief, however, is not confined to such fields. It is a term accommodating different concepts of the comparative roles of reason and authority in determining religious attitudes. As between Christians of different denominations, it admits a wide range of viewpoints on the degree to which one is, on the one hand, committed to the teaching voice of a Church and to conciliar definitions and credal confessions or, on the other hand, allowed to take one's own meaning out of the Bible and indeed to recognize only a minimal obligation towards the Scriptures in working out one's own religious position.

Freedom of opinion and the right to speculate are treasured prerogatives of all branches of learning and are indeed a condition of their progress. They have been fruitfully exercised in the Church from the beginning. But it has also been made clear from the beginning that theology, as the Catholic Church understands it, is basically the content of revelation as interpreted by the teaching voice of the Church under the guidance of the Holy Spirit. The criterion of what is to be believed is not a consensus of the learned, nor does the failure of scholars to reach a consensus—a situation often reached in the history of theology—mean that orthodox doctrine cannot be determined. One of the paradoxes of Christianity, as St Paul observed, is that its truth is liable to be folly in the eyes of learning and worldly wisdom. For the Catholic, theology cannot be equiparated with secular sciences: the faith may not be treated as a philosophy. The Church has received responsibility to interpret the deposit of faith, to identify what is consistent with it and what is not. It is for her to authorize the exposition of her teaching and she may not give general approval for its exposition independently of her.

A particular case for the autonomy of reason in matters of conduct as distinct from belief is sometimes made. It is asserted that only personal judgement on the merits of each moral issue can guide on whether an act may be done or not and that obedience to any external authority can never substitute for such personal judgement or constitute a truly moral act. The impression is sometimes given that even divine authority, although a presumption in its favour is recognized, cannot overrule the inalienable right of each individual to make up his own mind on questions of morality. This may be good natural-religion ethics but it does not accord with the system of guidance by God which revealed religion establishes.

There is no support in the Scriptures or in Church tradition for the view that all questions of conduct, as opposed to those of belief, are to be decided by personal assessment of each case. The indications are in the other direction. On two occasions when our Lord is questioned about the way to eternal life he refers to the commandments, going on in one instance to list them in the customary way (*Luke* 10:25-28; 18:20). It is evidently by way of accepting a ruling from God, and not through the individual's opinion that a Christian is typically to know what should be done. Our Lord sees his followers as 'observing whatsoever I have commanded you' (*Matt.* 28:20). His strict teaching on divorce in effect required that many of his hearers should go against their personal convictions; and their saying that marriage was therefore not expedient is a measure of how seriously they took his command. On the same subject St Paul goes against the majority view among both Jews and Gentiles by insisting that a married partner who separates must remain single, and he makes his ruling absolute by basing it on the Lord's command (1 *Cor.* 7:10-11).

Here again one must be careful not to overstate. To maintain the morality of obedience to lawful authority, even when one's own weighing of the ethical considerations would suggest a different conclusion, is not to discount the function of human intelligence in moral judgement. Apart from the right to repudiate obviously immoral or irresponsible exercises of power, human reason has a large part to play in the interpretation of the broad revealed principles of morality, and in addition the individual of necessity has much to decide in applying principles in particular cases. Catholics have always maintained that men can come to a considerable knowledge of moral law by reason; the predominant role of revelation has not with us led to disparagement of natural philosophy. It is true also that since morals relate to human actions they are more open to our discernment than things having directly to do with God—nevertheless, assessing correctly the factors for and against in an ethical problem is an exercise that often exceeds our capacities, as so many divergent findings demonstrate. We are in need of help here too: Christ is the way as well as the truth (*John* 14:6). It is not denying human intelligence its indispensable function in directing behaviour to say that the characteristic way of knowing what is right and wrong is, for the Bible, the word of God or of authority appointed by him, not personal opinion. Of the Pharisees and scribes in authority over the Jews, Christ told his followers to 'practise and observe whatever they tell you' (*Matt.* 23:3). St Paul knows of a law written in the heart of every man (*Rom.* 2:15) but the moral portions of his letters impose many peremptory and exact instructions on what should be done and what avoided. The Church has always exercised this function.

The whole system of revealed religion involves certain inroads on personal autonomy in regard to both belief and behaviour, and at the same time constitutes an enrichment which can more than compensate for any sense of frustration. Although there are some differences of detail, the same general principles apply in the departments of belief and conduct. Each dogma for which belief is demanded imposes a moral obligation to an act of assent and, if the validity of each obligation had to be a conclusion personally arrived at, one should logically be as free to withhold belief from a doctrine thought to be unreasonable as from behaviour deemed unethical. We are asked to submit to the word of God by believing what we cannot understand: it is hard to see what greater indignity is involved in obeying commands whose ethical justification one cannot discern. The moral value of placing God's word above personal opinion, the element of creaturely religious submission, is similar in both cases; in both cases inability to appreciate the internal case for what is required heightens, not lessens the quality of the religious submission. Furthermore, to require as a condition for a moral act that everyone appreciates its rational basis, even after a ruling has been given on it in revelation or by authority warranted by revelation, instead of emancipating the human person would in practice for most people impose an additional and sometimes an intolerable burden. What comes in the name of liberty may work out as a new rigorism.

II

The framework within which Christian thinking operates is then something other than ordinary sources of information—experience, observation, reasoning, intuition, imagination. Characteristically, our religion relies not on what is home-made but on what is adventitious. This is true also of the other important area of human life—conduct. Action follows thinking. If Christianity does more than merely augment and clarify our self-gained knowledge concerning God and his will, if it conveys information that is new in substance, similarly in the province of doing, it communicates power that is more than a mere energizing or redeployment of our natural capacities. It gives help that is new in kind, of a higher order than anything found in nature. As complement to new knowledge, ability is given to live up to it: we are made 'a new creature' in two respects.

The help given for knowing and that given for doing have all the signs of the same parentage. The origin of what we know by faith, however, since it relates to things otherwise unknown, is openly indicated. Our living, on the other hand, is assisted by God's imperceptible work in the soul so that this influence may easily escape attention. We have to be at more pains in order to appreciate the second form of God's communication to us under the New Covenant. The gospel not merely tells us about salvation through Christ and summons us to accept this gift. It tells us that we need, and assures us that we may have an assistance that is outside the order of nature in accepting that summons and in every phase of living up to it. The works we do in approaching God on the new level—and first of all the preliminary acts of faith and repentance—need to be of a quality that bears some proportion to an end which, properly speaking, is the sole prerogative of God. Hence they must be God-assisted, God-elevated in a way that none of our other acts are influenced, although all of them require the Creator's concurrence.

The New Testament makes it clear that the unbeliever and the sinner in approaching God through faith and repentance are, however unconsciously, being moved by the direct action of God on the mind and will, which constitutes a special favour exceeding the ordinary dispositions of nature. God is operative in our salvation before ourselves: we are in his debt from the very outset of our journey to him. 'No man can come to me unless the Father who has sent me draw him . . . no man can come to me unless it be given him by my Father' (*John* 6:44, 46). St Paul repeatedly refers to the same truth: 'It is God who works in you both to will and to accomplish' (*Phil.* 2:13); 'by grace you are saved through faith, not of yourselves, for it is the gift of God' (*Eph.* 2:8).

It is a serious distortion of the Scripture and of Catholic teaching to treat the divine assistance accorded to our actions as merely the influence which our knowledge of Christ through the gospel narrative or other external sources exercise on us. Such an effect is no more than the natural inspiration or attraction any human being can exert on others, whereas grace is God touching and affecting the soul immediately as only he can do. To think of grace in naturalistic terms would be to reduce it to what is known as 'external grace'—natural occurrences which prompt towards good: it would be the end of grace as we have known it up to now.

God's stirring the soul to do good is directed towards a lasting endowment. This somehow transfigures its recipient in the direction of the divine likeness and somehow conditions the soul for its destiny of permanent supernatural closeness to God. 'Justice' or 'justification' or 'righteousness'—the last may be the term lest open to misapprehensions just now, although it carries its own disagreeable associations—are translations of a word used widely throughout the Old and New Testaments. Its meaning for St Paul in its various Greek forms has been the subject of much thorough investigation in recent years. Lucien Cerfaux writes, as summing up the Pauline teaching: 'the coming of justice and its permanent dwelling in us are accompanied by a profound transformation, which is not simply a new attitude towards God, but an ontological difference, in the way in which the ancient writers understood a change of nature'.[2] It is more than the obliteration of sin, something additional to the indwelling of the Holy Spirit. To speak of it as constituted by a complex of acts and dispositions of mind and will is to fly in the face of Scripture and Church Councils.

The state of grace has many aspects but it is essentially a gift, 'a benefit which is freely given',[3] and which has the effect of incorporating us into Christ as a member, part of a body which is his body (1 *Cor*. 12:27). Our Lord has spoken correspondingly of the relationship of branches to a vine (*John* 15:5). Both of these descriptions imply the constant and direct transfer to guidance and nourishment. We are reborn into a new life, a continuing new state (*John* 3:5-6; *Tit*. 3:5). We 'have to put on Christ' (*Gal*. 3:27). 'It is no longer I who live but Christ who lives in me' (*Gal*. 2:20). Christ has proclaimed himself the life as well as the way and the truth (*John* 14:6). St Peter says we are made 'partakers of the divine nature' (2 *Pet*. 1:4), a saying to be considered with St John's 'we shall be like him for we shall see him as is' (1 *John* 3:2), as reminding us of the final goal to which sanctifying grace is directed.

To lose sight of or keep out of the way or do less than justice to such extraordinary language would be treason to a vital part of Christianity. From the beginning there is a solid line of tradition which insists that the Scriptures mean that a kind of divinization comes with grace. 'Deification' is a term found in a long series of Fathers from St Irenaeus to St Augustine. St Thomas writes: 'the only begotten Son of God desiring to make us partakers of his Godhead, assumed our nature that, having become man, he might make men to be gods'.[4] Councils of the fifth and sixth centuries as well as Trent have committed the Church to the understanding of sanctifying grace as a permanent and inherent enhancement of the soul's condition, having the character of a gratuitous divine favour.

In regard to faith, the Scriptures, as we have seen, emphasize the preponderant part God plays, by saying that to human wisdom our belief is folly, and that it shows up best when it is not associated with human wisdom and therefore has, to all appearances, to work alone. Our indebtedness to God is brought out similarly in regard to grace by showing that it is characteristic of it to partner human weakness. This point is made several times in the second epistle to the Corinthians. St Paul is told when he prays for relief in his affliction: 'My grace is sufficient for you, for my power is at its best in weakness' (12:9). 'When I am weak then I am strong' (12:10), he goes on to say; and again: 'If I must boast I will boast of the things that show my weakness' (11:30), and 'our sufficiency is from God' (3:5). Grace does not depend on natural qualities of character in the recipient any more than faith depends on human intelligence. The generous readiness of Christ to forgive the sinner—'I did not come to invite virtuous people but sinners' (*Matt.* 9:13)—exhibits in practice this partiality for the under-endowed.

Here too, however, God's greater share in what is effected does not discount the human contribution. Small as this is, relatively speaking, and itself the gift of God, in being the product of actual grace, the voluntary effort of the human will in reaching out to God is essential. The value and the need of good works in attaining the state of grace, as of the free assent of the intellect in faith, was maintained firmly by Catholics as against those who would assert the complete corruption of man through original sin and the consequent worthlessness of all that man could contribute to his own saving. This is another of these counterpoises we must be careful not to forget in singling out for special attention the predominant features in the structure of our relations with God.

These matters are not being raised now in the interest of old controversies but because of their actual pertinence. The conveying of knowledge and of power directly from God is what constitutes Christianity; we need today to be clear on their import and on the place they hold in the divine scheme. The same kind of tendencies to evade and ignore and repudiate which have been looked at in relation to faith are evident also in much that is being written about grace. Reference has been made in passing to an extreme liberal theory which would reduce grace to a relationship between God and man on a par with the influence one human being can exercise on another by evoking love and enthusiasm. There are other currents of opinion moving in the same direction, whose effect can only be to minimize or destroy our appreciation of the dispensation of grace. Going with them would place us in practice in the position of rejecting what God has offered to us.

The world is becoming busier every day with short-term objectives to satisfy urgent demands. Material developments, improvement in standards of living, prevention of diseases, provision against famine, keeping the earth from polluting and atoms from exploding—the list is every day lengthening of what we should and must do in the interests of survival. God forbid that anyone speaking in the name of Christianity should minimize the need for every effort that can be made for the improvement of man's earthly condition: in the midst of so much affluence there is more need than ever for such exertions. The works of mercy are to form the matter of the Last Judgement and a cup of cold water given in Christ's name will not go without reward. Christian social endeavours, though increasingly forthcoming, can never be enough.

There is so much to be done in the world that we are in very near danger of thinking, with bebelievers, that worldly matters are our chief or our only concern. Religion, some suggest, cannot be preached by the Church with a good conscience until she has seen to the establishment of justice in the world. That the Church is too much involved in politics is a familiar charge: today there are those who prescribe for the Church the political systems they consider it her vocation to advocate as alone satisfactory, and who deplore her emphasis on the spiritual. The Church's realization of her social responsibilities and of her duty to promote justice has never been clearer than in our time and as opportunity affords it will no doubt be more fully expressed. But the degree of her involvement in political movements and the priority to be accorded to secular and debatable issues on which she has received no command from the Lord cannot be considered without reference to the attitude adopted by our Lord himself on such matters.

Although our Lord gave a great part of his time to alleviating human distress and sowed seeds of love and compassion that were to manifest themselves in the course of time in many social reforms and re-orientations of thought, he punctiliously avoided being involved in any political or constitutional movements. Being embroiled in popular upheavals would deflect attention from the infinitely more important revolution of the spirit with which he was concerned. He paid the tribute money claimed by Rome and refused to say that giving it was unlawful. He ran away from those who wanted to make him king, as he had rejected Satan's temptation to earthly power, turning down thereby the unlimited opportunities he might have had of remedying the obvious social evils of his time and establishing the exemplar of the just society. To suggest that when he declared a special blessing on those who hunger and thirst after justice he was referring to the redress of social injustice is simply to misconstrue his words. Promoting justice between man and man is indeed fulfilling the purposes of God, but in the beatitude in question it is the pursuit of supernatural justification, of 'holiness' that is commended. When asked to arbitrate on property rights he refused, saying: 'Man, who has made me a judge or divider over you?' (*Luke* 12:14). Our Lord puts first what is first in his own and in his apostles' calling. His followers are not to worry about food and drink and dress or run after what the pagan world seeks but to set their minds first upon the kingdom of God (*Luke* 12:31). It is an emphatic declaration of priorities, not of course a sanction for quietism in the ordinary business of life.

The objectives which revelation requires us to aim at as overwhelmingly the more important, are spiritual, supernatural, other-worldly. The gospel, the good tidings which we are committed to announce, relate to the forgiveness of sin through the redemptive act of Christ and the possibility of attaining something greater than the human heart could aspire to in the vision of God in the after-life. We must continue to proclaim these truths in the Christian Church. We should be in a position to counter jeers about man's eternal destiny being merely an invention to palliate present injustice, by showing that we are not only concerned with the after-life but are active in innumerable practical ways in making this world a better place. The point is that while we are so engaged we must not leave our foremost

duty undone or relegated to second place. As with the truths of
faith, we meet here the temptation of human respect in an acute
form today. It is easy, because it requires only a negative attitude,
to be evasive or virtually silent about what is singular in our faith
and therefore apt to make us seem at odds with a sophisticated
world. But the good news of the gospel is grace and we are
responsible for delivering its message without adulteration or
dilution—even though worldly wisdom will always tend to regard
it as folly, as belonging to the world of magic and fairy-tale.

Integral Christianity needs proclaiming all the more clearly in
times when people are very prone to think of man's needs in
terms of this life merely and to regard deprivation of the world's
goods as the only evil. There is plenty of evidence in our disturbed
world that even among the worldly-minded the peace that the
world cannot give is needed and missed. So much the greater,
then, is our opportunity and duty to testify to what comes to us
through Christ and even in this life. Grace is more than preparation for an eternal destiny: the Holy Spirit comes to comfort and
sustain us in present difficulties. In so far as men can for a time
find reasonable content in what the world offers, they are at best
not fulfilling the purposes of God or attaining what we are
offered by him. Rejecting the supernatural is analogous to
declining to exercise the higher part of our nature and opting for
an animal or vegetable existence.

As much as anything else, modern man needs to be reminded
that he possesses a spiritual nature which cannot find complete
satisfaction in anything or everything in this world. A deprivation
that is not measurable in terms of currencies or calories is the
great disability of our day. Our Lord spoke in words of passionate
regret and tenderness of the hunger and emptiness of which
men insist on making themselves victim: 'Come to me all you that
labour and are heavy laden and I will give you rest' (*Matt.* 11:28);
'How often I would have gathered thy children together even as
a hen gathers her chickens under her wing and ye would not'
(*Matt.* 23:37); 'He that comes to me shall never hunger and he
that believes in me shall never thirst' (*John* 6:25). He is the bread
of life (*John* 6:48), the light of the world (*John* 8:12), the shepherd
(*John* 10:14), the door of the sheepfold (*John* 10:7). Our desperate

need of God and his capacity and urgent desire to help us are fundamental truths that require to be preached incessantly in an age which despite its achievements—and perhaps because of them —is short-sighted and narrow-minded.

Antipathy to living by the grace and favour of God is showing itself in a tendency to depreciate the means by which his help is obtained. Devotion, spiritual exercises, personal private prayer are sometimes positively discouraged—an attitude that may be less evident because of emphasis on external and community worship. Little is made of what our Lord most commended and what is the essence of any true converse with God: contact with him in secret, the kind of prayer which is to be unceasing, adoration in the spirit and in truth as distinct from its concentration in holy places (*Matt.* 6:6,18; *Luke* 18:1; *John* 4:23). The extent of things one may pray for is questioned on philosophical grounds—as if St Thomas had not long ago shown that the divine eternity means that God has always been cognisant of our petitions-to-be and his providence has taken account of them. (It is typical that old objections should be revived and their answers left out of sight.) It is forgotten too that prayer is not merely petition, it is communion of the soul with God in several ways. However we may individually fall short in practice in this matter, to assert and defend neglect in regard to prayer—to make people feel insecure about the pieties which are the very respiration of faith—is to incur a responsibility which no pleading for legitimate change can lighten.

An extreme form of this attitude has gained some notoriety in connection with the slogan 'God is dead', which is apt to mean at least that many may now act and shape his life on the assumption that God does not and must not be expected to intervene in our favour. To say that 'God makes us know that we must live as men who can get along without him' is to say the direct contrary to what Christ says. Other movements towards the exinanition of the Christianity of Christ are found in the theory that Christianity must be freed from 'the religious premise', that Christianity is 'a secular movement'.

Writing in this vein may affect the outlook and living of many who would reject such extremes of language. Disuse of communication with God is all too easy a habit. It would not only starve our life of supernatural union with God: it would deprive us of our strongest resource in ordinary living and in the management of the world's affairs. The God who is interested in the fall of a sparrow and in the grass that withers tomorrow, is interested in the worldly affairs in which our spiritual lives are enmeshed. He has told us so. We may legitimately ask him who cares for every aspect of our welfare to influence the course of external events favourably. The psalms are full of petitions for everyday needs and our Lord instructed us to pray for temporal and material help: 'give us this day our daily bread'. To believe that we can now manage the world's affairs by ourselves is to have done with the religion of the Bible.

Unwillingness to admit our inadequacy, to shake off this inveterate desire that 'man shall be like gods' is at the root of much of our present day I-will-not-be-indebted-to-God complex, of the tendency to eliminate from faith and grace, so far as we retain them in name, an element which is central. Sometimes the subtraction takes rather disarming and deceptive forms. Another old objection that is re-appearing is that since Christianity offers rewards for virtue it is merely a mercenary contract and can claim no moral excellence: in order to be good, conduct must be unselfish. But in fact Christianity, in teaching that we must love others as we love ourselves, puts altruistic love on a level with self-love. The advantage of others is not to be willed merely in one's own interest—the only further motivation it receives is one it holds in common with self-love—reference to the divine will as ultimate objective. But in this matter account must be taken also of a larger truth.

Unselfish love of God, perfect charity, as it has come to be called, has always been commanded as the highest of virtues. But it is not the only virtue, even within the field of love. God, the infinite source of all our being, is also the only source of our ultimate happiness. It is the divine plan that man should attain that destiny, and consequently it is part of the plan that he should aim at it and desire it. God wishes man to be happy with him, and, that man should not look forward to enjoying such happiness would be like refusing a favour from a friend or steeling oneself to gain no pleasure from it. No one would defend treating a human benefactor so churlishly as to refuse to gratify his wish to give pleasure. It is a subtle assertion of self-sufficiency and pride to take up such an attitude towards God. Worse than that: it is an inversion of the true order of things. God is the giver, we creatures are *ex hypothesi* receivers. He is the source of our self-realization in joy: he expects us to accept this objective order of things, to find and therefore to look forward to happiness in him. We may not reverse roles and insist that in our relations with him we shall only regard ourselves as givers. God expects of us the natural reaction to favours of children whom, in another of those paradoxes that are meant to challenge our self-conceit, he several times made our exemplars. In these days the admonition 'unless you turn and become like children, you will never enter the kingdom of heaven' (*Matt.* 18:3) is liable to be drowned by voices proclaiming that our generation has grown to full manhood.

These then are traits that govern and define our religion in the most comprehensive way and at the same time impart a special quality to its constitutive elements. Ignoring these matters or failing to recognize their central importance would be more than relinquishing certain doctrinal positions. It would be altering the whole nature of Christianity since these are the elements that distinguish and identify it. In relation to suggested alterations in faith and morals they provide an obvious check on such developments as are inconsistent with fundamental principles and may be calculated to destroy what is essential. That so many currents of opinion today run counter to the very framework and design of our religion is evidence of the pressures which, under the guise of legitimate and desirable progress, are at work against its supernatural character and in the direction of reducing it to the scale of this world and to the level of natural religion.

That this kind of exercise in analysis is necessary just now is the best apology one can offer for a certain starkness that inevitably attaches to discussing Christianity in terms of abstract principles. Concentrating on fundamentals cannot but leave much unsaid that would give flesh and warmth and life to what may seem theoretical and formal. It is important to see the general scheme and system of our religion as a conveying of knowledge and of energy which condition all our relations with God. At the same time one should acknowledge always the limitations of theology which deals in analogies and inferences rather than descriptions, and relate to laws and generalities and the mechanics of God's ways with man rather than the actual experience towards which everything else is in fact directed. In the world of the spirit we can never offer those exact pictures the imagination craves.

We must not fail to realize, however, that the net effect in practice of the features that are seen as characterizing Christianity is not in the direction of formalizing and abstraction. The trend of modern thought, even where religion is still honoured, is towards autarchy, towards pushing God more and more out of our actual living, thinking and working. The principles we have dwelt on act in the contrary direction. They bring God more fully than any other system of thought has imagined into all we are and do. And the relationship is not merely mediated by things said and given: it is direct and personal. God comes into our lives in the most intimate way, giving us the most immediate help, establishing with us bonds which only extravagant language can attempt to match. Our religion, as it works out, is love, confidence, piety; not philosophical formulae.

The dogma of the supernatural does not mean that our religion remains in the domain of the ethereal and transcendental. It comes to life in the mind and heart of the believer. God-become-man is not just a mystery of faith, it is the Person of the crib and the cross, the most loving and beloved of men. Grace is not just a term covering certain unfathomable changes wrought in the soul by God; it is in practice our daily support and comfort in difficulties, peace of mind and confidence, the hand of a loving Father leading his children and enabling them to do more than they find it in themselves to do. Our whole supernatural relationship with God, however encroaching its demands may appear, is suffused with love which transforms both commands and obedience. Mortification of the intelligence and will are requirements that must attend on the intervention of God as revealer and sanctifier in what in euphoric moments we like to think of as this warm kind world where all we know is all we need to know. But the chief sacrifice involved is not sacrifice on our side. It is significant that our supreme act of worship is not an offering of ourselves or of anything we have made or own but of the Victim God himself has provided for us. The pattern of counterpoint is everywhere. We give his own giving.

Select Bibliography

W. H. Abbott-J. Gallagher (ed.), *The Documents of Vatican II*, London-Dublin-Melbourne 1967.

B. W. Anderson (ed.), *The Old Testament and Christian Faith*, New York 1969 (1963).

The Archbishop of Canterbury (ed.), *Lambeth Essays on Faith*, London 1969.

R. Aubert, *Le Probléme de l'acte de foi*, Louvain 1950.

H. Bouillard, *Logique de la foi*, Paris 1964.

H. Bouillard, *The Knowledge of God*, London 1969.

Guy de Broglie, *Revelation and reason*, London 1965.

J. P. Burke *et al.*, *The Word in History: The St Xavier Symposium*, New York 1966.

J. Coventry, *The Theology of Faith*, Notre Dame, Indiana 1968.

M. C. D'Arcy, *Belief and Reason*, London 1944.

G. Ebeling, *Word and Faith*, Philadelphia 1963.

G. Ebeling, *God and Word*, Philadelphia 1967.

H. Fehmers (ed.), *The Crucial Questions*, New York-London 1969.

J. Hick, *Faith and Knowledge*, London 1967.

J. Hick, *Philosophy of Religion*, Englewood Cliffs, N.J. 1963.

R. Latourelle, *Theology of Revelation*, New York 1966.

R. Latourelle, *Theology: Science of Salvation*, St Paul Publications 1969.

L. Malevez, *Pour une théologie de la foi*, Paris 1969.

R. Mitchell *et al.*, *Faith and Logic*, New York 1958.

L. Monden, *Faith: Can Man Still Believe?* New York 1969.

J. Mouroux, *I Believe*, London 1959.

H. H. Price, *Belief*, London 1960.

E. Schillebeeckx, *God and Man*, London 1969.

H. Zarnt, *The Question of God*, London 1969.

Notes

INTRODUCTION

1. Pastoral Constitution on the Church in the Modern World, art. 21. (All quotations from Council documents are taken from *The Documents of Vatican II*, ed. W. M. Abbott, London-Dublin-Melbourne 1967.)

PROBLEMS OF BELIEVING TODAY

1. See J. Pieper, *Die Überlieferung*, Munich 1969.
2. In the Preface to W. Wickler's *Sind wir Sunder?*, Munich 1969.
3. 'Dimensions of Meaning' in *Collection*, Papers by Bernard Lonergan, S.J., edited by F. E. Crowe, S.J., London 1967, 266-7.
4. See André Frossard, *God exists, I have met him* (E. tr. M. Villiers),
5. *Veille de fête je reste un Barbare*, Paris 1962.
6. See Viktor E. Frankl, *Man's Search for Meaning: an Introduction to Logotherapy* (E. tr. Ilse Lasch), London 1968.
7. In *Der Spiegel*, 5 Jan. 1970, 79-84.
8. *Der Teil und das Ganze: Gespräche im Umkreis der Atomphysik*, Munich 1969; see p. 195 for what follows.
9. *Introduction to Christianity* (E. tr. J. R. Foster), London 1969.
10. *Ibid.*, 43.

DIVINE REVELATION: SOURCE OF MAN'S FAITH

1. See Leslie Dewart, *The Foundations of Belief*, New York 1969.
2. *The Teaching of the Catholic Church*, ed. Karl Rahner (E. tr. G. Stevens), Cork 1967, 36.
3. See Gordon D. Kaufman, 'Two Models of Transcendence. An Inquiry into the Problem of Theological Meaning', in *The Heritage of Christian Thought*, *Essays in Honor of Robert Lowry Calhoun*, ed. Robert E. Cushmann and Egil Grislis, New York 1965, 182-96.
4. See Ulrich Duchrow, *Sprachverständnis and biblisches Hören bei Augustinus*, Tübingen 1965; Donald H. Nash, *The Light of the Mind. St Augustine's Theory of Knowledge*, Kentucky 1969.
5. See The Dogmatic Constitution on Divine Revelation, art. 1)-13, *Documents of Vatican II*, 120-21.

6. I have quoted and commented on this text of St Augustine in *The New Life of Grace*, London-New York 1969, 129-30.

7. *Ibid.*, 99, and see also Appendix, p. 361, for more references to this and similar topics.

8. For further implementation of this theme, see my book on grace, the chapter 'Redemption, Grace and Church', *op. cit.*, 58-86.

9. See Piet Schoonenberg, 'God en mens: een vals dilemma' (God and man: a false dilemma) in: *Hij is een God van mensen*, Twee theologische Studies, 's Hertogenbosch 1969, 9-48. An English translation is being prepared.

10. See *The New Life of Grace*, *op. cit.*, 282-316.

11. On Divine Revelation, art. 8, *Documents of Vatican II*, 116.

12. The term 'motion', here and throughout this paper, is used in the sense of the word *motio* employed by St Thomas (also by St Ignatius) in describing the divine activity in the soul through grace. [Editor's note.]

13. *Ibid.*, art. 1-10, *Documents of Vatican II*, 111-18.

14. '. . . and we now await no further new public revelation before the glorious manifestation of Our Lord Jesus Christ.' On Divine Revelation, art. 4, *Documents of Vatican II*, 113.

15. See Malcolm Hay, *Failure in the East, Why and How the Breach between the Western World and China First Began*, Wetteren (Belgium) 1956.

16. See P. Fransen, 'How Can Non-Christians Find Salvation in Their Own Religion?' in *Christian Revelation and World Religion*, ed. Joseph Neuner, London 1967, 67-122; Y.-M. Congar, 'Ecclesia ab Abel', in *Abbandlungen Uber Theologie und Kirche*, Festschrift für Karl Adam, Dusseldorf 1962, 79-108. This historical survey is written in French.

17. Karl Rahner, 'Gotteserfahrung heute', *Theologische Akademie*, VII, ed. K. Rahner and O. Semmelroth, Frankfurt 1970. He writes: 'wenn heute deutlicher wird und zwar auch innerhalb des lehrhaften und institutionellen Christentums dass diese Gotteserfahrung (allerdings als radikal und richtig interpretierte) wirklich der Kern des Christentums und auch die lebendig bleibende Quelle dessen ist, was, reflektiert, "Offenbarung" heisst, dann kommt dadurch das Christentum nur radikaler und deutlicher zu seinem eigenen Selbstverstandnis', p. 24.

18. See note 13.

19. On Divine Revelation, art. 7, *Documents of Vatican II*, 115.

20. See for the Church and the sacraments two chapters from *Intelligent Theology*, I, London 1967: 'The Idea of the Church and the Holy Trinity', 40-66, and 'Sacramental Grace and the Divine Indwelling', 91-125. In relation to the problem of conscience, see 'Freedom of Conscience'', *Intelligent Theology*, III, 1969, 115-44.

21. On Divine Revelation, art. 11, *Documents of Vatican II*, 119.

22. See my 'Man and Freedom', in *Man before God, Readings in Theology*, New York 1966, 69-89.

23. See *The Word in History*, ed. T. Patrick Burke, New York 1966: Karl Rahner, 'Theology and Anthropology', 1-23, and Edward Schillebeeckx, 'Faith Functioning in Human Self-Understanding', 41-59.

24. Paul Touilleux, *Introduction à une théologie critique*, Paris 1967, with an enthusiastic Foreword by Fr M. D. Chenu, the famous French Dominican.

25. G. Moran, *Scripture and Tradition*, New York 1963; *id.*, *Theology of Revelation*, New York 1966; *id.*, *Catechesis of Revelation*, New York 1966; and in dialogue with the paper by Schillebeeckx, quoted in footnote 23, 'The God of Revelation', 'God', *Commonweal Papers 1*, 85 (1967) 494-505. One may quote in relation to these problems the famous French philosopher Paul Ricoeur, 'Contribution d'une reflexion sur le langage à une théologie de la Parole', *Revue de Théologie et de Philosophie* 18 (1968) 333-48.

26. Louis Monden, *Faith, Can Man Still Believe?*, New York 197. The original Flemish title seems more expressive. It might be translated: The Language in which we Understand God.

CHRISTIAN FAITH AS PERSONAL RESPONSE

1. See J. Sperna Weiland, *New Ways in Theology* (E. tr. N. D. Smith), Dublin 1968, 213 ff.

2. See Denzinger-Bannwort 822, 824.

3. Denz. 798

4. See J. Lacroix, *Meaning of Modern Atheism* (E. tr. G. Barden), Dublin 1965, 104 ff.

5. Denz. 1789.

6. Denz. 1795.

7. Denz. 2145.

8. See the Dogmatic Constitution on Divine Revelation, art. 5, *Documents of Vatican II*, 113.

9. *Summa Theologiae* 2—2.2.1.

10. *Ibid.*, 2—2.1.1.

11. *Ibid.*

12. *Ibid.*, 2—2.2.2.

13. G. Kittel, ed., *Theological Dictionary of the New Testament*, VI (E. tr. G. W. Bromiley), Grand Rapids, Michigan 1968, 187.

14. *Ibid.*

15. Kittel, *op. cit.*, 195-6.

16. See C. H. Dodd, *The Interpretation of the Fourth Gospel*, London 1968, 86.

17. See Karl Barth, *Evangelical Theology: an Introduction* (E. tr. G. Foley), London 1965, 95.

18. For a survey of what historical research can verify about these events see, for the Old Testament, M. Noth, *Geschichte Israels*, Gottingen, 6th ed. 1966; for the New Testament there is ample bibliography on the quest for the historical Jesus—e.g. James Robinson, *A New Quest of the Historical Jesus*, London 1959.

19. See, e.g., James Hastings, *Dictionary of the Bible*, Edinburgh, revised ed. 1963, 553.

20. See Wilken's contribution in W. Pannenberg *et al.*, *Revelation as History* (E. tr. P. Granskow), New York 1968.

21. See Rolf Rendtorff, 'The Consent of Revelation in Ancient Israel', in Pannenberg, *op. cit.*

22. See my 'New Thinking on Revelation', *Herder Correspondence* 6 (1969) 302.

23. Buber can give this impression, that he is thinking of such a purely intersubjective relationship between man and God, and it is this impression that wins him most of the criticism he has received. See M. Buber, *I and Thou* (E. tr. R. G. Smith), Edinburgh 1947. But the impression is probably not correct. See what he says about the universe becoming language in God's response: cf. pp. 11, 75, 100, 103.

RELIGIOUS EXPERIENCE AND CHRISTIAN FAITH

1. One thinks here of Ritschl and his followers. See K. Barth, *From Rousseau to Ritschl*, London 1959, 391 ff.

2. E.g. N. Smart, *Philosophers and Religious Truth*, London 1964, 139.

3. Penguin Books, Harmondsworth 1959. The book was first published (in German) in 1917.

4. *Ibid.*, 21; cf. 56-64.

5. Richard R. Niebuhr, *Schleiermacher on Christ and Religion*, London 1964, p. 194, footnote 29.

6. Otto, *op. cit.*, 30.

7. *Ibid.*, 40, 42.

8. *Ibid.*, 45.

9. *Ibid.*

10. *Ibid.*, 33.

11. *Ibid.*, 45.

12. *Ibid.*, 50.

13. *Ibid.*, 63.

14. Niebuhr, *loc. cit.*

15. Introduction by R. Otto to F. Schleiermacher, *On Religion: Speeches to its Cultured Despisers*, New York 1958, xviii; Karl Barth appears to have accepted the same interpretation of Schleiermacher— see Barth, *op. cit.*, 190.

16. Niebuhr, *op. cit.*, p. 76, footnote 2, and p. 194.

17. Cf. A. Vergote, *The Religious Man: a psychological study of*

religious attitudes, Dublin 1969, 32.

18. E.g. Barth, *op. cit.*, *passim*, On the results of the attacks by Barth and Brunner see Niebuhr, *op. cit.*, 175-6 and, especially, p. 177, footnote 3.

19. Niebuhr, *op. cit.*, 178.

20. L. Dupré, 'Toward a Revaluation of Schleiermacher's Philosophy of Religion', in *The Journal of Religion*, Vol. 44, No. 2 (April 1964), 103.

21. Cf. Niebuhr, *op. cit.*, 126.

22. *Ibid.*, 121.

23. F. Schleiermacher, *The Christian Faith*, Edinburgh 1928, p. 7, § 3, 2, note.

24. See note 15 above.

25. Cf. Otto's introduction to *On Religion* . . ., xii.

26. Dupré, *art. cit.*, 100: 'For Schleiermacher, as for Kant, full consciousness results from an opposition between subject and object. Yet in the post-Kantian tradition of Fichte and Schelling, he holds this opposition to be preceded by a timeless moment of identity.'

27. *On Religion* . . ., 44.

28. *Ibid.*, 41.

29. Cf. Dupré, *art. cit.*, 102.

30. *The Christian Faith*, § 5, 4 (pp. 22-4); cf. § 32, 1 (pp. 131-2).

31. *Ibid.*, § 5, 3 (p. 21).

32. *Ibid.*, § 4, 3 (p. 15).

33. Niebuhr, *op. cit.*, 122.

34. Cf. *Ibid.*, 184.

35. *The Christian Faith*, § 15, 1 (pp. 76-7).

36. *Ibid.*, § 5, postscript (p. 25).

37. *Ibid.*, § 4, 4 (p. 17).

38. *Ibid.*; cf. Niebuhr, *op. cit.*, 185.

39. Cf. *The Christian Faith*, § 5, postscript (p. 25).

40. Barth, *op. cit.*, 335.

41. *The Christian Faith*, § 16, postscript (pp. 81-3).

42. *Ibid.*, § 16, 1 and 2 and 3 (pp. 78-80).

43. *Ibid.*, § 19 (pp. 88-91); cf. Niebuhr, *op. cit.*, 149, 153, 167.

44. Niebuhr, *op. cit.*, 164.

45. Dupré, *art. cit.*, 100.

46. This is part of what worries Barth about Schleiermacher's theology—see Barth, *op. cit.*, 330, 351. Barth's treatment of this issue can be confusing because he is unwilling to treat Christianity as a 'religion'. See our discussion of this point below.

47. L. Feuerbach, *The Essence of Christianity*, London 1854, Ch. 1, § 1 (p. 9).

48. A. Fonck, 'Möhler', in *Dictionnaire de Théologie Catholique*, X, col. 2057.

49. J. A. Möhler, *Symbolism: or Exposition of the Doctrinal Differences between Catholics and Protestants as evidenced by their symbolical writings*, London 1894, Book I, ch. 5, section 38 (pp. 278-80).

50. See the interesting article by N.-D. O'Donoghue, 'Is there a Christian Sense?', in *The Irish Theological Quarterly*, Vol. 37, No. 1 (Jan. 1970) 3-23.

51. J. Ratté, *Three Modernists: Alfred Loisy, George Tyrrell, William L. Sullivan*, London 1968, 34.

52. Denz. 3477.

53. Cf. Ratté, *op. cit.*, 149; J. J. Heaney, *The Modernists Crisis: Von Hügel*, London 1969, 201. An adequate study of 'immanentism' would, of course, need to show the profound truth which it contains. For instance, Alfred Loisy's brilliant study *The Gospel and the Church* (London 1908, 256-7), suggests that 'an unseen necessity' which is 'unconscious' but 'not therefore accidental' operates in Catholic piety and affects theology and doctrine. It is this which lies behind the development of dogma. On the basis of this account Loisy is quite right in claiming that the 'conceptions which the Church presents as revealed dogmas are not truths fallen from heaven, and preserved by religious tradition in the precise form in which they first appeared' (*ibid.*, 210).

54. Cf. R. Aubert, 'Modernism', in *Sacramentum Mundi: An Encyclopedia of Theology*, *IV*, London 1969, 100. This aspect can be related to Loisy's final view that there is no normative external revelation, so that nothing controls the evolution of Christianity but the evolution of humanity towards full consciousness; and so humanity itself becomes the *depositum fidei*. See Ratté, *op. cit.*, 131-4.

55. Cf. Ratté, *op. cit.*, 35.

56. Cf. E. Schillebeeckx, *The Concept of Truth and Theological Renewal*, London 1968, 12.

57. G. Tyrrell, *Through Scylla and Charybdis or The Old Theology and the New*, London 1907, 229. For Tyrrell's defence of his 'immanentism' see his *Mediaevalism: A Reply to Cardinal Mercier*, London 1908, 110-12.

58. G. Tyrrell, *Christianity at the Crossroads*, London 1907, 94.

59. *Through Scylla . . .*, 278-9.

60. *Ibid.*, 289.

61. G. Tyrrell, *Lex Credendi: a Sequel to Lex Orandi*, London 1906, viii; cf. Schillebeeckx, *op. cit.*, 10-11.

63. Schillebeeckx, *op. cit.*, 11-12.

64. *Ibid.*, 10, 12.

65. *Lex Credendi*, 128.

66. *Ibid.*, 16.

67. *Ibid.*, 181.

68. *Ibid.*, 25-42.

69. *Ibid.*, ix.

70. *Ibid.*, 54.

71. *Ibid.*, 49.

72. *Ibid.*, 14.

73. *Ibid.*, 252.

74. *Ibid.*

75. Ratté, *op. cit.*, 188; cf. Schillebeeckx, *op. cit.*, 20-21.

76. Denz. 3475.

77. Heaney, *op. cit.*, 129; Aubert, *art. cit.*, 102.

78. J. Revière, 'Modernisme' in *Dictionnaire de Théologie Catholique*, X, col. 2045: 'Voilà pourquoi il semble permis de dire sans temerité que la phase du modernisme aigu est close, et qu'une nouvelle poussée dans ce sens n'est guère conforme aux vraisemblances de l'histoire.'

79. K. Rahner and H. Vorgrimler, 'Modernism', in *Concise Theological Dictionary*, London 1965, 290.

80. Cf. B. Lonergan, 'Theology in its New Context', in *Renewel of Religious Thought (Theology of Renewal*, Vol. I)—*Proceedings of the Congress on the Theology of the Renewal of the Church, Centenary of Canada 1867-1967*, edited by L. K. Shook, C.S.B., New York 1968, 45.

81. See, for instance, K. Barth, *op. cit.*, *passim.* An interesting analysis and critique of Barth's position is to be found in H. Bouillard: *The Knowledge of God*, London 1969, 11-62; also in J. Macquarrie, *God-Talk: An Examination of the Language and Logic of Theology*, London 1967, 41-50.

82. Cf. B. Lonergan, 'The Natural Knowledge of God', in *Proceedings of the 23rd Annual Convention of the Catholic Theological Society of America*, Washington D.C., 17-20 June 1968, 54-69. This point is also a major theme in L. Gilkey, *Naming the Whirlwind: the Renewal of God-Language*, Indianapolis and New York 1969.

83. B. Lonergan, 'The Natural Desire to see God', in *Collection: Papers by B. Lonergan, S.J.*, edited by F. E. Crowe, S.J., New York 1967, 92.

84. 'The History of Religions as a Preparation for the Co-operation of Religions', in *The History of Religions: Essays in Methodology*, edited by M. Eliade and J. Kitagawa, Chicago 1959, 132-60.

85. *Ibid.*, 142.

86. 'Faith and Beliefs' (public lecture) 1969, section 2; cf. 'Theology and Man's Future' (Sesquicentennial celebrations of St Louis University, public lectures 1968) to be published in a book edited by J. Padberg; 'The future of Christianity' (public lecture 1968. What follows is dependent on Lonergan's treatment.

87. *Ibid.*

88. 'Faith and Beliefs', section 3.

89. *Ibid.*

90. E.g. M. Eliade, *The Sacred and the Profane: the Nature of*

Religion. New York 1961; *Patterns in Comparative Religion*, London 1958; *Myths, Dreams and Mysteries—the Encounter between Contemporary Faiths and Archaic Relaties*, London 1968; *The Quest: History and Meaning in Religion*, Chicago 1969.

91. E.g. *Patterns of Comparative Religion*, 417, 429 f.; *The Sacred and the Profane, passim.*

92. Cf. B. Lonergan, 'The Absence of God in Modern Culture' in *The Presence and Absence of God* (The Cardinal Bea Lectures), edited by C. F. Mooney, New York 1969, 164 ff.

93. B. Lonergan, 'Faith and Beliefs', section 4.

94. Cf. B. Lonergan, 'Dimensions of Meaning', in *Collection . . .*, 262-3.

95. Cf. Vergote, *op. cit.*, 38.

96. The phrase was coined by the German sociologist Georg Simmel. This reference and our account is based on B. Lonergan's 'The Future of Christianity', cf. 'The Absence of God in Modern Culture'.

97. See, for instance, the interesting account of such essential changes, in the classical anthropological study by Ruth Benedict, *Patterns of Culture*, London 1935.

98. Cf. B. Lonergan, 'The Transition from a Classical World View to Historical Mindedness' in J. E. Biechler (ed.), *Law for Liberty: the Role of Law in the Church Today*, Baltimore 1967; *id.*, 'Theology in its New Context', 37-41; *id.*, 'The Absence of God in Modern Culture', *passim.*

99. E.g. Macquarrie, *op. cit.*, 195-230.

100. Cf. B. Lonergan, *Verbum: Word and Idea in Aquinas* (ed. D. Burrell), London 1968, 59, 140; *id.*, *Insight: A Study of Human Understanding*, 2nd ed., London 1958, 552 and *passim.*

101. For a very clear analysis of the scope and limits of this knowledge as defined by the First Vatican Council see B. Lonergan, 'The Natural Knowledge of God'; also Bouillard, *op. cit.*, 20-24.

102. I am indebted to an unpublished tract on revelation by F. E. Crowe, S.J., for this approach. I am unable here to do more than hint at the rich theology he provides.

103. *The Two and The One*, 205: The symbol has 'a capacity for expressing paradoxical situations or certain patterns of ultimate reality that can be expressed in no other way'.

104. P. Ricoeur, *The Symbolism of Evil*, Boston 1969, 16: '. . . the symbol . . . assimilates us to that which is symbolised without our being able to master the similitude intellectually.'

THE ACT OF FAITH IN THE REFORMED TRADITION

1. 'Nunc iusta fidei definitio nobis constabit si dicamus esse divinae erga nos benevolentiae firum certamque cognitionem, quae gratuitae in Christo promissionis Veritate fundata, per Spiritum sanctum et

revelatur mentibus nostris et cordibus obsignatur' (III, 2, 7).

2. 'Cognitio divina erga nos benevolentia . . .'.

3. '. . . perpetuam esse fidei relationem cum verbo, nec magis ab eo posse divelli quam radios a sole, unde orientur . . .' (III, 2, 6). And, 'Tolle igitur verbum et nulla iam restabit fides' *ibid.*

4. '. . . perpetuum esse fidelibus certamum cum sua ipsorum diffidentia' (III, 2, 17).

5. 'Sola est fides quae in nobis caritatem primum generat' (III, 2, 41)

6. 'Si quis dixerit, homines iustificari vel sola imputatione iustitiae Christi vel sola peccatorum remissione, exclusa gratia et caritate, quae in cordibus eorum per Spiritum Sanctum diffundatur atque illis inhaereat aut etiam gratiam qua iustificamur, esse tantum favorem Dei: A.S.' (Denz.-Schonm. 1516).

7. 'Haec doctrina post me obscurabitur.' Se non è vero, è ben trovato.'

8. 'Firmus ergo fidei status non erit, nisi in Dei misericordia sistatur' (III, 2, 29 s).

9. *Fides qua* refers to the (subjective) act of faith as distinct from *fides quae* which refers to the (objective) content of faith.

10. 'Fidem quae humanae salutis initium est, Ecclesia catholica profitetur, virtutem esse supernaturalem qua Dei aspirante et adiuvante gratia ab eo revelata vera esse credimus' (Denz-Schonm. 3008).

11. *The Documents of Vatican II*, p. 113, note 7.

12. *A New Catechism*, London 1966, 289-90.

13. K. Rahner and H. Vorgrimler, *Concise Theological Dictionary*, London 1964, 164.

14. *A New Catechism*, 292-3.

THE HISTORICAL CHURCH AS MEDIATOR OF FAITH

1. *S. Theol* 2-2, 1.1.

2. See J. N. D. Kelly, *Early Christian Creeds*, 2nd ed. London 1960, 152.

3. Published in Dublin, Sydney, Dayton Ohio, 1968.

4. *S. theol.* 1-2, 94, 4.

5. See Pope Paul VI's encyclical, *Mysterium Fidei*, articles 23-4.

6. D. Bonhoeffer, *Letters and Papers from Prison*, edited by E. Bethge (E. tr. R. Fueler), London 1967, 178.

7. *Ibid.*, 156.

8. *Ibid.*, 152.

9. *Ibid.*, 172.

10. *Ibid.*, 167.

FAITH AND REASON

1. Monsabre: quoted in *The Teaching of the Catholic Church*, edited G. D. Smith, London 1948, 12.

2. I am using this distinction not precisely in the sense in which it was used by Bertrand Russell, who introduced it to philosophy, but in the more colloquial sense explained by Jane Austen in chapter 21 of *Sense and Sensibility* where Lucy says 'I have not known you long, to be sure, personally at least, but I have known you and all your family by description a great while; and as soon as I saw you I felt almost as if you were an old acquaintance.'

3. *Dogmatics in Outline*, London 1949, 23.

4. *A Grammar of Assent*, London 1891, 109.

THE WAY OF FAITH

1. Vincent of Lerins, *Commonitory* (E. tr. H. Bindley), London 1922, 54.

2. Lucien Cerfaux, *The Christian in the Theology of St Paul*, London 1967, 425.

3. Cerfaux, *ibid.*

4. *S. theol.* 1-11, 112, art. 1.